# Divine Place of Discovery as a Bittersweet Flower

Almarean Ward Whitfield

TRILOGY CHRISTIAN PUBLISHERS
*Tustin, CA*

TRILOGY

Trilogy Christian Publishers
A Wholly Owned Subsidiary of Trinity Broadcasting Network
2442 Michelle Drive
Tustin, CA 92780

*Divine Place of Discovery as a Bittersweet Flower*

Copyright © 2024 by Almarean Ward Whitfield

Scripture quotations marked ESV are taken from the ESV® Bible (The Holy Bible, English Standard Version®), copyright © 2001 by Crossway Bibles, a publishing ministry of Good News Publishers. Used by permission. All rights reserved.

Scripture quotations marked ISV are taken from The Holy Bible: International Standard Version. Release 2.0, Build 2015.02.09. Copyright © 1995-2014 by ISV Foundation. ALL RIGHTS RESERVED INTERNATIONALLY. Used by permission of Davidson Press, LLC.

Scripture quotations marked NASB are taken from the New American Standard Bible® (NASB), Copyright © 1960, 1962, 1963, 1968, 1971, 1972, 1973, 1975, 1977, 1995 by The Lockman Foundation. Used by permission. www.Lockman.org.

Scripture quotations marked NIV are taken from the Holy Bible, New International Version®, NIV®. Copyright © 1973, 1978, 1984, 2011 by Biblica, Inc.™ Used by permission of Zondervan. All rights reserved worldwide. www.zondervan.com. The "NIV" and "New International Version" are trademarks registered in the United States Patent and Trademark Office by Biblica, Inc.™

Scripture quotations marked NKJV are taken from the New King James Version®. Copyright © 1982 by Thomas Nelson. Used by permission. All rights reserved.

Scripture quotations marked NLT are taken from the Holy Bible, New Living Translation, copyright © 1996, 2004, 2015 by Tyndale House Foundation. Used by permission of Tyndale House Publishers, Inc., Carol Stream, Illinois 60188. All rights reserved.

All rights reserved, including the right to reproduce this book or portions thereof in any form whatsoever.

For information, address Trilogy Christian Publishing
Rights Department, 2442 Michelle Drive, Tustin, CA 92780.

Trilogy Christian Publishing/ TBN and colophon are trademarks of Trinity Broadcasting Network.
For information about special discounts for bulk purchases, please contact Trilogy Christian Publishing.

Trilogy Disclaimer: The views and content expressed in this book are those of the author and may not necessarily reflect the views and doctrine of Trilogy Christian Publishing or the Trinity Broadcasting Network.

10 9 8 7 6 5 4 3 2 1
Library of Congress Cataloging-in-Publication Data is available.

ISBN 979-8-89333-467-8
ISBN 979-8-89333-468-5 (ebook)

# Dedication

Having the esteemed opportunity to present this book in memory of my parents, the late Mr. and Mrs. James and Mearlon Ward, is a blessing. Although they are not physically here, their teachings and graciousness continue to inspire me. Their very essence exemplified the epitome of born-again believers who lived by precept and example. Graced with love, selflessness that endowed a spirit of giving culminated with acts of kindness that swelled far beyond family ties. Their openhandedness and influence generated the construction of the local church (Household of Faith), and their beloved benevolence spread well into the community.

Dad and Mom truly embraced the scripture, "It is more blessed to give than to receive" (Acts 20:35). Their declaration was, "We are blessed to be a blessing." They helped those in need in any way they could. More importantly, you did not have to be in need to be recipients of their caring and sharing. They served people with bountiful resources that God had blessed them with. It was done in the spirit of love "just as a good neighbor."

Reared in a Christian home and growing up in church provided me with an essential spiritual foundation. In both settings we were taught the unadulterated Word of God. At an early age, my parents instilled discipline, foundational principles, dignity, and interpersonal skills. Dad and Mom would emphasize the benefits of trusting God and putting Him first and how to love people in-spite-of. Also, with practical applications, they further expressed these principles (recalling a few):

- Whatever you do or whatever job you have, always do your best.
- Be the best that you can be.
- Don't half do nothing" (anything).
- Always stand for right, even if you have to stand by yourself.
- Just know that God will always be with you.
- When God tells you to do something—do what God say do regardless what man might say.

Those wholesome principles guided me from day-to-day.

Just as I reflect on a couple of precious memories (there are many) during early childhood, I remember in my parents' bedroom placed over their bed was a gold frame plaque (blue background, gold lettering) inscribed, "The Golden Rule: Do unto others as you would have them do unto you." Oftentimes, my parents would quote and emphasize the importance of that principle and how to apply it in everyday life, emphatically indicating that it is our job to treat everyone right and with respect. Even when I felt mistreated, Daddy's response was, "You do right." He would further utter an old cliché, "Charity begins at home, then spread abroad." Subsequently, I have always tried to practice the Golden Rule in my daily walk.

Another precious memory recalled: Every evening at dinnertime, Daddy would share excerpts of God's Word, graced with divine wisdom as it relates to life's situations. In turn, Mom would share practical examples that correlated with Daddy's teaching/lecture. Q&A sessions would commence with my siblings and I. All questions were answered according to biblical principles. This truly was a family affair and we (children) gained a wealth of knowledge and understanding.

Of course, my siblings and I grew tired of the long lectures (pretty much) every evening at dinnertime. Nevertheless, we had no choice but to listen. After dinner, one to two days out of the week, we would gather around the piano. Daddy would play the piano and always commence leading spiritual songs. The very first song would be, "Don't Forget the Family Prayer," and we all joined in. Subsequently, we began singing a succession of songs. These tender times were precious and we enjoyed fellowship with one another. Singing, rejoicing, and oftentimes learning new gospel songs. As a result of that spiritual and musical experience/collaboration, a few years later, our enthusiastic singing group, "The Ward Sisters," came into fruition.

Precious memories such as these made an indelible impact on my life. Undoubtedly, their legacy represents a lasting hallmark of Christian and family values. In addition, because of Dad and Mom's unwavering love for God (in obedience) we produced immense love for humanity.

Lastly, my sincere testimony is to echo that their love, godly teaching, and establishment of a Christian foundation blessed and helped shape me to be who I am today. They had faith for me when I was unable to produce it for myself. Without them, there would be no me. Without me, there would be no book. For these reasons, it is a magnificent honor to dedicate this manuscript to their loving and precious memory.

## "Tribute to Momma"

Thank God for Momma, now she has gone
mother bowed down and prayed for me
when she was at home.
She intervened on the scene,
petitioning heaven by-all-means.
Her prayers touched heaven
asking God for blind eyes to be awakened
and trust God and not be taken by austere situations
that will pass—realizing God's promises are the only
thing that will last.
God is monumental; intentional in word and deed,
He will assuredly meet the need.
Momma taught,
Just believe that God will bring me out
without a doubt
while angels applaud with a shout!

When
spiritually awakened, scales fell from my eyes
and I realized that God is always on my side.

I am a winner and on arrival
to tell my truth, as a survival.

# Foreword

"I am Alpha and Omega, the beginning and the ending, saith the Lord, which is, and which was, and which is to come, the Almighty" (Revelation 1:8).

"And the Spirit and the bride say, Come. And let him that heareth say, Come. And let him that is athirst come. And whosoever will, let him take the water of life freely" (Revelation 22:17).

"For the prophecy came not in old time by the will of man: but holy men of God spake as they were moved by the Holy Ghost" (2 Peter 1:21).

God knows:
My makeup:
"Even every one that is called by my name: for I have created him for my glory, I have formed him; yea, I have made him" (Isaiah 43:7).

My name:
"Listen, O isles, unto me; and hearken, ye people, from far; The LORD hath called me from the womb; from the bowels of my mother hath he made mention of my name" (Isaiah 49:1).

My heart:
"For the word of God is quick, and powerful, and sharper than any two-edged sword, piercing even to the dividing asunder of soul and spirit, and of the joints and marrow, and is a discerner of the thoughts and intents of the heart" (Hebrews 4:12).

Who else could know me better?

To that I say, "God, the Holy Spirit" serves as my "Foreword."

# Preface

At birth, when the trail of life begins is to embark upon open-ended bittersweet journeys. Life's journey unfolds into a wide-range of possibilities, challenges, and surprises to embrace or reject. By the same token, lifecycle perspective is comprised of willpowers: a) aflame with a fearless desire (internal hope) to achieve the best life by making prudent decisions; or, b) by having a tendency to neglect to pursue one's divine place by making reckless decisions.

My journey, captured in the experiences of life, is somewhat mirrored in an original poem titled, "Discovering My Place" (Chapter 1, Ref. Session: "My World"). I realize the bittersweet experiences of life are, in some way or the other, common to humankind, which is all-embracing in this manuscript.

In the early 2000s, I awakened at an early morning hour; poetical inspirations had bombarded my thoughts in three intervals of sleep. The first couple of times, I turned on the lamplight and scribbled on a pad that lay dormant on the nightstand. Therewith, my heavy eyes outweighed my will and I slumbered. The third time, the blissful words were coming so rapidly and audibly in my spirit; this time my will outweighed my flesh. Subsequently, I resorted to another bedroom and began to complete the poem, "Discovering My Place."

Fortunately, the poem reappeared after being misplaced for several years. And thankfully, around 2007, the Holy Spirit impressed upon me to finish what I initially started—drafting a manuscript. By being obedient, positive adjustments were made to resume the task. Furthermore, it involved drafting additional sections of the manuscript to personify the poem. I was filled with enthusiasm and compassion to share personal experiences, spiritual insight, and biblical teachings that were imparted to me over the years. What is more, this manuscript is graced throughout with (original) poetic inspirations to uplift the heart, soothe the soul, and refresh one's spirit. Nevertheless, this undertaking did not come without apprehension and a world of obstacles/setbacks. Unfortunately, there were intervals of delay; months (on and off) that stretched into years. Keeping the scripture Philippians 4:13 close to heart: "I can do all things through Christ which strengthened me," reinvigorated the passion and drive to move forward.

"And the Lord answered me, and said, Write the vision, and make it plain upon tables, that he may run that readeth it" (Habakkuk 2:2).

My sincere trust is that this book is reflective of life, in general, that can be applied on all levels, spiritual/secular arenas, and in varied situations. At some point in time, everyone (like myself) has found themselves in a place of discovery (i.e., self/class, spiritual/carnal; social/political; professional/academic, etc.), stained with rejections, identity crisis, bias, questionable choices, and the list goes on. Confronted with such threats, prudent decision-making is paramount for constructive resolution. It is essential to decide which chosen path/road to take in finding your true place of divine destiny.

# Acknowledgments

**To the Triune Godhead:**

First and foremost, I would like to express special homage to the Triune Godhead: God the Father, God the Son, and God the Holy Spirit. The Holy Trinity, embodied with awesome glory and power, bestowed upon me the gift, wisdom, grace, and inspiration to write this book. During this process, it would not have come to fruition except by the auspices of divine power and execution. With that, I am eternally humble and grateful to God.

**To my spouse:**

Loving thanks go out to my dearest husband, Cornealius (Neal). Upon undertaking this writing assignment, you believed and encouraged me to embrace the challenge. As the project progressed (overwhelmed with countless obstacles), you emphasized the importance of trusting God for strength to cross the finish line. Your steadfastness, words of comfort and sound advice helped to reinforce my faith and go forth in prayer and perseverance.

**To our children/grandchildren:**
Cornealius, Jr. (Nick), Michael (Mike), and Sheree. Thanks for believing in me and for your overall support. Sheree, I sincerely appreciate your dramatic sense of humor that kept me laughing throughout this venture. Grandchildren: Thank you as well.

**To my siblings and their spouses:** Elaine W. Stafford, Eld. Louvenia W. Straughter, Mattie W. Smith (Timothy), Marjorie W. Dumas (Ernest), David Ward (Ruth), and Annie (Ann) W. Haynes. You have always supported me in whatever endeavor I undertook. Ann, you stated, "This book can be used as a spiritual reference book." Thanks to each of you and much love.

**Church family/affiliation:** Bishop Dr. Lorenzo Moore, Presiding Prelate; (Lady/Mother Delois Moore); Bishop Dr. Gus C. Ford, General Secretary, College of Bishops; my Pastor, David M. Northcutt; (Lady Renita Northcutt); National & Diocese Officers; pastors; and fellow members of the House Of God Saints In Christ, Inc. This live organism (Christian organization) is where I began my Christian journey. The Ecclesiastical circle potently teaches the unadulterated Word of God.

It provides spiritual support, wise counsel, encouragement, and training that continues to enhance my spiritual development as a Christian. I am truly obliged.

**My Nieces and Nephews:**

I would like to express my genuine thanks to Janice Ellis and your beloved husband (the late Walter Ellis) for volunteering to read my manuscript and to give feedback on the quality of the product. During that time, Ellis was not at all at his best, but with his caring and selfless spirit, he was the first to volunteer to read the manuscript, with exuberance. I remembered he said, "Auntie, I'll be glad to read your manuscript." Both of you reported that this manuscript is godsent and how it touched your hearts. Janice, I remember telling you that someone asked, "Did you have a ghost writer?" And I said, "Not at all." You, in turn, said, "Tell them yes you did, the Holy Ghost!" And that, my dear, is the truth. Thanks again for your selfless act of kindness during your busy schedule and solemn challenges.

**Nieces and Nephews:**

There are too many of you to name, but I only want to say thank you for your well wishes, prayers, and for cheering me on regarding this endeavor.

**Special Friends:**

Sister (Mother) Martha Collins (ninety-two years young). I call you, Sis. Collins, because my parents adopted you (goddaughter) into our family over forty years ago. Over the years, we truly became family outside our church family. Your home is my home and my home is your home. Thanks for your spiritual support, open door, and encouragement over the years. Your wise counsel, sense of humor, straight talk, and the spirit of witnessing of the goodness of God will be forever cherished.

**My sincere appreciation** goes out to Mattie Fluitt, Diane Harding, Lois Thomas, and Carol Grisby Pollard for being there for many years during the good times and bad times. Your spiritual encouragement, laughter, and heart-to-heart dialogues kept it real—in keeping with the Word of God. When you learned of my endeavor, you were excited about what God is doing through me; you encouraged and lifted me in prayer.

**Former Coworkers:**

Thanks to everyone—Cleasie Hickson, Hylah Jordan, Teresa Kolodziej, Sheila Jones, and Iris Sinkfield—for your support and encouragement throughout this venture. You were very attentive to listening to some of the original poems. Being inspired, you gave a thumbs up. Teresa, you were so moved by a particular one, stating that it needs to be aired in the paper, etc.

**Thank you** to LaDarryl "L.A." Hollingsworth of Creative Notions Design Group for helping establish my book's feel and social media presence.

**Trilogy Christian Publishing (TBN Network):**
Shout out to the Trilogy Christian Publishing/TBN Network team Rhett Harwell, Trilogy Acquisitions Executive; Media Services; and the Production Team, who worked diligently making it possible to present the finished product, *Divine Place of Discovery as a Bittersweet Flower* at this precious time in history. Thank you, dearly.

*Come...*
   *Journey with me from*
         *Sun*down *to Son*rise!

# Introduction

WHEN was the last time you went on a great trip? On this journey, birth certification serves as a boarding pass to obtain life's itinerary dating from cradle to grave. Adverse climate changes are certain, so it is paramount to be properly dressed. Therefore, spiritual armor is essential to pack, as well, while journeying in this natural environment. Undoubtedly, this amazing journey will most definitely test one's character—feelings, sense, beliefs, and surroundings/conditions.

All ABOARD, GET SET, LET'S GO! We are on our way to the Divine Place of Discovery. What a sight to see, things to do, places to go, and lessons to learn while traveling on life's pathway. Life's journey is filled with wonderful realities, coupled with bittersweet experiences. All-encompassing liberties versus constraints; triumph versus defeat; oceans of opportunities; hills of happiness; prosperity; and joyful sounds. Undesirably sundry days of sadness, disappointments, and chilling challenges oftentimes appear to overshadow better days, such is life. Dare not forget the crossroad of decisions to ponder and reconcile while endeavoring to reach the divine place that God ordained.

> "Storing up for themselves the treasure of a good foundation for the future, so that they may take hold of that which is life indeed" (1 Timothy 6:19, NASB).

Life is symbolic of a bittersweet plant (flower). According to the definition of *bittersweet* by vocabulary.com, "The adjective bittersweet does not just refer to taste. It can also describe a blend of emotions that are sweet but also tinged with sadness... The feelings and memories you have make you simultaneously happy and sad, and are therefore bittersweet."[1] A *bittersweet ending* is still ending on a high note, but one that is mixed with sadness and nostalgia. Often, such endings are the result of the plot, making a completely happy ending impossible. (Looked at objectively, some happy endings have more things lost or irrevocably broken than some bittersweet endings).

Countless people are discouraged and disengaged regarding spiritual intervention and emotional recovery due to the absence of hope while on the trail of life. With no urgency to navigate and escape Satan's entrapment, which is detrimental in discovering one's purpose, known peace and wholesomeness are drastically fading in the eclipse of darkness. Due to the disobedient/ corruptible nature of Adam/Eve, defiance emerged, permeating the inborn fabric of humanity into a darkened state imposing bittersweet journey. In-the-midst of adverse circumstances, a treasure chest of divine purpose, glorious promises of prosperity, and abundant life are available while in pursuit of discovering that divine place. The adversary's deliberate, methodical assault is sanctioned towards humanity to hinder, abandon, and conquer the divine purpose and plan of God (by whatever means necessary).

To that end, herewith was designed a spiritual journey-script (Word of God) to navigate through this pilgrimage. Thusly, this penned literature is to explore the day-to-day life challenges, struggles, temptations, and fears by overcoming plights comparative to natural roads and landscapes, deserts, and culturally modified places that we experience and enjoy.[2,3] This is accomplished from three perspectives: first, second, and third persons (i.e., my, your, and our, respectively). Discovering My, Your, and Our divine place is pivotal to having a successful journey and an expected end. In discovering these distinctive personal places, significant questions must be assessed and individually answered. a) Where is my Place? b) What is my Purpose? and c) When is my time to Pursue/Propel? In essence of this manuscript, these questions will be fully addressed.

Be it known, we are pilgrims passing through this life en route to eternity. This spiritual compass/road map serves as a guide in making sound choices versus bad decisions to reach divine destiny rather than a detrimental end. As you travel on this journey, Matthew 7:13–14 speaks of two gates: a) strait gate/narrow, and b) wide gate/broad.

> "Enter ye in at the strait gate: for wide is the gate, and broad is the way, that leadeth to destruction, and many there be which go in thereat: Because strait is the gate, and narrow is the way, which leadeth unto life, and few there be that find it."

The straight gate brings to mind the conceptual meaning of the phrase "walking the straight and narrow." That is, exhibiting good behavior, on the up-and-up at all cost, and so forth. By entering the narrow gate (spiritual), we become "apples of God's eye." Along the way is a well of living water designed to refresh one's soul when you reach those dry places. Planted are fruit trees of the spirit, servings of milk and meat of the Word of God for babes in Christ and seasoned saints, respectively. The table is set for those who hunger and thirst after righteousness. More importantly, enter the sacred place to have holy communion with God. Alternatively, there is a broad gate (secular) unflinching with little or no interest in divine intercession. As you pick and choose, at the upmost, the bountiful Bread of Life is there for the taking. It is available for everybody, even those who may feel like nobody, to eat thereof. The Word of God can save anybody when your eyes are open (insight) and your heart is sure. Aside from that, there are spiritual gifts to be discovered hidden in the treasure chest of the issues of life as you search the depths of your soul.

> "I will give you the treasures of darkness And hidden wealth of secret places, So, that you may know that it is I, The LORD, the God of Israel, who calls you by your name" (Isaiah 45:3, NASB).

However, make no mistake about it, the journey comprises challenges and plights while en route to divine destiny. While under pressure, these tests/trials and impasses are strengthening stepping stones (in disguise), designed to equip and propel one into divine destiny when relenting is not an option. To be successful in traveling this spiritual journey, make sure you "put on-the-whole armor of God, that ye may be able to stand against the wiles of the devil," as referenced in Ephesians 6:11. The prevailing threat is to be exposed to unhealthy intellectual and philosophical environments that lead to diminishing spiritual deficit. Being in the right place endorses purpose, and the pursuit will yield a fruitful harvest in the Kingdom of God, simultaneously bringing revitalization and prosperity within the natural capacity of one's existence. The point is, to take hold of a divine place is to be intentional, intellectually aware, spiritually enlightened, and have a wholesome natural place (environment) to work out your soul's salvation and purpose.

> "Wherefore, my beloved, as ye have always obeyed, not as in my presence only, but now much more in my absence, work out your own salvation with fear and trembling" (Philippians 2:12).

What is more, oftentimes one of the primary culprits that rob our divine destiny is a distraction that culminates into escalating trepidation, procrastination, and abandonment. It is like hot toasted desert sand and blistering sun. It commences like puffs of white clouds cascading into the sky where climatic changes force the clouds to slumber and disrobe. Thusly, the sky fades from her silvery blue tent into a dark horizon that paralyzes. Sounds like distraction, right? Regardless of your make-up, (i.e., socioeconomic status, ethnicity, gender, religious beliefs, age group, etc.), the journey (whatever path you take) is peppered with life's challenges—tests, trials, threats, and some failures. Borderline victories?

Yes. Someday those "almost made it" attempts will be won! At some point on the journey, it is essential to reassess your route (situation), redirect your path (actions), and reengage your spirit (beliefs/will) to ensure the road you are traveling is a sure foundation.

> "He will be a sure foundation for your times, abundance, and salvation, wisdom and knowledge—the fear of the LORD is Zion's treasure" (Isaiah 33:6, ISV).

# Contents

Prologue. Possibilities and Pilgrimage of Pursuit....xxxi

Poem. "Journey".................................................xxxix

Chapter 1. My World—Discovering My Place ............... 1

   Poem: "Discovering My Place" ................................. 1

   The Bud (Bittersweet Flower).................................... 3

   Place of Discovery (New Love, Mission, and Clarion Call).................................................................. 8

      Poem: "Color Me Rainbow" ................................13

   Safely in His Arms..................................................15

      Poem: "U-2" ......................................................... 21

Chapter 2. Your World—Discovering Your Place ....... 23

   Investigative Discovery ........................................... 23

   Where is My Place?................................................. 29

   Poem: "Reflections" ................................................ 46

   What is My Purpose?.............................................. 48

      Prayer Walk (Steps) ............................................. 54

      Poem: "Shekinah Glory"..................................... 57

   When is My Time to Pursue/Propel? ......................60

      Poem: "With God, You Can" .............................. 65

      Poem: "Life" ......................................................... 68

Chapter 3. Eye of the Storm........................................ 72

   Waterlogged ............................................................ 72

   The "Calm Effect" ................................................... 75

Poem: "Trapped in the Storm" ............................ 77
Shaken to Rest ........................................................80
Inwardly Secret Storm ......................................... 81
　Poem: "Loneliness" ................................................. 83
Outward Appearance ........................................... 85
Outwardly/Bubbling Mask (Association vs. Assimilation) .............................................................. 87
　Poem: "God's Grace" ................................................91

## Chapter 4. Weather the Storm ....................... 93
Steadfast Power....................................................... 93
　Obtainability............................................................. 97
　Responsibility........................................................... 99
　Endurability............................................................101
　Poem: "Touch of Greatness" ............................. 107
　Poem: "Rainwater" ...............................................110

## Chapter 5. Our World—Discovering Our Place ........ 112
National Proclamation ........................................112
　Preamble to the Constitution of the United States............................................................................. 114
　Spiritual Directive................................................. 117
　Poem: "Together We Stand"............................... 120
　Excerpts of the Preamble (Narrative)............... 122
　World of Interrelation ........................................ 133

## Chapter 6. Predestined Plan of God.............136
Divine Discovery ...................................................136
　Divine Place ..........................................................138

- God's Divine Purpose Disclosed ........................ 139
- God's Order................................................................ 140

Chapter 7. Dusk to Dawn ............................................. 142
- SONdown................................................................... 142
- Divine Pursuit/Forfeited (The Bud—Fall of Man) ........................................................................ 142
- Paradise Lost ........................................................... 144
- SONRISE..................................................................... 147
- Hope of Glory (The Flower/Jesus, The Risen Savior) ...................................................................... 147
- Prelude to Salvation ............................................. 149
- Life-Rousing Questions ....................................... 152

Chapter 8. The Bright and Morning Star ................. 154
- Crown of Life Bestowed........................................ 154
- Poem: "We the World" .......................................... 156

Epilogue .......................................................................... 159

Endnotes ........................................................................ 168

Bibliography.................................................................. 172

PROLOGUE

# Possibilities and Pilgrimage of Pursuit

**Possibilities**

For the sake of this communication and the perspective in which it is written, to the commitment and steadfastness of all Christian Soldiers whose feet are shod with the preparation of the gospel of peace, serving in the Army of the Lord through the winding roads of Possibilities. On this pilgrim's journey, inevitably the believer, and likewise unbelievers, will encounter various opportunities (i.e., artistic, entrepreneurship, religious and secular industries, etc.) to explore, channel, and develop in the quest of life, liberty, and the pursuit of happiness. Without doubt, encompassing bittersweet experiences that are unavoidable. Just know that a vast range of unlimited potential is internal to bring into fruition, which will be a blessing to others. This will be accomplished by staying focused when navigating through the trail of life.

Metaphorically, the winding test tube roads of life (places you've been/situations in) are depicted as various landscapes:[4]

a) Natural landscape, such as mountains, hills, valleys, rivers, sand, plains, and plateaus, etc.

b) Desert landscape—hot, dry, sandy soil, dunes

c) Cultural landscape—landscape that people have modified

(Metaphorical landscape descriptions are referenced throughout this manuscript.)

> "Thus says the Lord: 'Stand by the roads, and look, and ask for the ancient paths, where the good way is; and walk in it, and find rest for your souls.' But they said, 'We will not walk in it'" (Jeremiah 6:16, ESV).

While on life's journey, whether traveling a natural road or spiritual path, there are numerous routes available to choose. Prior to deciding the route, a decisive place of destination is essential to fulfill one's mission. It is vital to count up the cost for the journey—taking into consideration the good, bad, and ugly. Let us be real—every decision may not be the right decision. And when making the right decision, sometimes things still go awry. But regardless of whatever course is taken, unexpected detours, roadblocks, potholes, and bridge outages are probable on this journey. Trust the spiritual compass and know that God's grace is sufficient.

**Pursuit**

In the process of discovering one's divine place, it is paramount that distinction is made between the forces of good and evil; light and darkness; bitter and sweet. Being submissive and held hostage to the "cares of this world, and the deceitfulness of riches, and the lusts of other things" stampedes spiritual rationality in one's life (Mark 4:19). Giving rise to declining cerebral capacity to reason, minimizes atrocious behavior which renders a smoke screen of spiritual normality. This eroding decision-making process paralyzes the effort of establishing an objective solution that ultimately leads to an unprofitable journey without substance. Mental struggles and indecisions commence to flood the mind. Oops! Another spiritual roadblock; spiritual warfare at play. The adversary enacts this tactic by forming unhealthy secular collaboration by way of carnal wills and desires that arrest the mind, spirit, body, and soul. The stronghold is designed to drain every ounce of strength to hinder spiritual camaraderie within to combat this attack. As a result, and if not careful, we will succumb to debilitated choices, procrastination (false timetable), and desolation of the spirit, rather than illumination of the mind that will transform into new life and spiritual perspective.

> "And be not conformed to this world: but be ye transformed by the renewing of your mind, that ye may prove what is that good, and acceptable, and perfect, will of God" (Romans 12:2).

Through one's volition and a consecrated spirit, invoked with celestial intervention, entrenched in the heart of the mind, is the ability to choose divine prosperity over man's failure—obedience vs. rebellion. Consequently, the result is salvation vs. damnation, heaven vs. hell. Encountered with a smorgasbord of options, catapult decisions to ponder—whether to enjoy worldly channels consumed with undesirable compromise and pernicious actions sanctioned by Satan's intentional desire and objective, or to put on spiritual traveling shoes for the journey. As spiritual warfare surfaces within, inner battles between mind, heart/soul, and spirit expose damaging clouds of carnality that rolled back the sun (Son) that commenced to shine (in our heart) on a rainy day. In times like these, whatever the dilemma, etc., rebuke the enemy and be steadfast, trusting in the Word of God knowing that God's Word will not return unto Him void.

"Then spake Jesus again unto them, saying, I am the light of the world: he that followeth me shall not walk-in darkness, but shall have the light of life" (John 8:12).

In the natural aspect, the physical road, *artery* is defined as "a major route of transportation into which local routes flow," according to *The American Heritage Dictionary*.[5] Whereas, in spiritual light, a way was made regarding humanity's itinerary to travel the main "artery," which will be addressed in the section "Dust to Dawn" of this manuscript. Let us be clear: the surest route on life's journey commenced during the foundation of the world. God's divine plan and purpose were initiated and remain steadfast for humanity to thrive when God is foremost.

On the other hand, and in keeping with this concept, one of the most important organs in the human body is the heart. It is so important in that one cannot survive without it. Miraculously, the heart is in the chest cavity that houses the lifeblood flowing from God to humanity. It inherently serves as the spiritual reservoir (soul cavity) where the issues of life flow. Issues of life are an equal opportunity employer and come with no disparity of quality, right? No one has to apply but is automatically enlisted.

"A man's heart deviseth his way: but the LORD directeth his steps" (Proverbs 16:9).

Undergirded in the issues of life are countless esthetic situations where the initial presentation appears to be lovely and to shine like gold, impinged in hiding the dross that will eventually transpire, which is the backdrop of life's screen play. But overcoming power is ensued in the orderly divine inner peace that is available according to one's volition.

In any case, unceremoniously, life can thrust people into uncontrollable situations that force them to seek for an "overpass" that can lift them over their burdensome experiences. Although, time after time, the issues of life cause many to travel on costly and speedy roads such as "throughways" and "highways" of life. Living high in carnality (carnal pleasures) and "bypassing" spiritual serenity. Farther up the road, choosing to take the "turnoff" where there is no "through street" to the heavenly "path." In so doing, many become stuck (in the fast lane), wasting valuable time.

"Keep thy heart with all diligence; for out of it are the issues of life" (Proverbs 4:23).

As the timetable of life continues to turn, many find themselves in a "maze" they can easily get lost in. A "maze" is equivalent to being blindfolded. You continue to go around and around for a long time without reaching an open door and/or a successful destination. Sounds much like an "open road," traveling with no goals, plans, or purpose in mind. Is this really living or just merely existing? In the majority of cases, if there is no reckoning of the mind and a deliberate will to reassess and redirect one's actions, it will ultimately lead to a "dead end." Why not take the route of the heavenly "freeway" where salvation is free? Jesus paid the price over two thousand years ago for believers to be able to sit in heavenly places with Him while living your best life.

> "A highway shall be there, and a road, and it shall be called the Highway of Holiness. The unclean shall not pass over it, but it shall be for others. Whoever walks the road, although a fool, shall not go astray" (Isaiah 35:8, NKJV).

> "And hath raised us up together, and made us sit together in heavenly places in Christ Jesus" (Ephesians 2:6).

Refusal to take the heavenly "freeway" will cause one to end up on a "tollway" where payment is enforced to drive on. Journeying without the Savior, Jesus Christ, one may experience overwhelming trouble that causes unbearable heartache and spiritual desolation—immoral, immortal, and illegal bankrupt, and eventually one may pay with one's life. In every situation, God has given believers the power to overcome all adversities and a way to escape. The same holds true for unbelievers when Jesus is made Lord of their life.

> "For whatsoever is born of God overcometh the world: and this is the victory that overcometh the world, even our faith" (1 John 5:4).

## POEM:
## "JOURNEY"

Life's journey is filled with whispers,
loud noises, melodious sounds.
Cries that still the night, hoping somehow
everything will be all right.
Enduring preoccupied spaces...then, dead silence!

Silence of the unknown—dare to groan
broken hearts, empty places
endless contemplation; time wasted
culminating into lapse of time.

Time is a journey and journey is time.
Entwine with each other;
Unless valued and sing your song,
You will never know when you are traveling wrong.

Dressed for the journey from head to toe
Believing God will make a way before, I know.
Traveling shoes, LORD, got on my traveling shoes.
As the Negro spiritual declares it,
be honored to walk in it.

Stage is set for pursuit of happiness
to be valor or victim of weariness

in the arena of the world's
pugnacious progressiveness.

Get ready to tell your story as you grow old
as life unfolds.
To be captured in history, on a dime,
marked by time.

Time is of the essence. Life is time; time is life.
Fastly moving, you are right on time.
Already on board, that my friend,
when your story began.

Moment baby cried when taken from mother's womb
Placed in crib; mouth, bottle, and bib.
Waiting for mom's body to heal.

Growth and development on the journey
Happy go lucky; bouncing baby jolly!
Inhaling and exhaling, marking time;
realizing God has set an appointed time.

Time is passing in a zoom!
Soon will be time to make more room
for the trail of life echoes gloom
if have not prepared to breathe the fresh air
of His glorious presence with no despair.

### DIVINE PLACE OF DISCOVERY AS A BITTERSWEET FLOWER

In your travel from the room,
over time, you will make way to the tomb.

Where are you going?
What are you doing with your time?
Time is precious. Cannot see it, Oh, my goodness,
the body feels it!
The worn, the torn; strong to weak
Bittersweet.
Life to death, short or long;
Daylight to darkness infiltrates the air~
Somewhere, Anywhere
Bomb!
You are gone.

CHAPTER 1

# My World— Discovering My Place

**POEM:**
**"DISCOVERING MY PLACE"**

There are many places I have been
Other places I just did not feel comfortable in.
There are places where I thought I wanted to be,
But in those places, I just could not be free!
There are places where I was not invited
And many did not appear exciting.
There are other places where I wanted to labor,
In order to work out my own soul salvation.
My gifts and talents were not needed—
Too many others were already seated.
There were positions where I wanted to serve...
I was told, "They are already reserved."
There is ministry I wanted to embrace,
I was told in so many words, "I didn't fit the qualification stage."

By whose standards? Man's standards or God's standards?
Nevertheless, I have been seeking God for an answer!
These were places that failed to accommodate me,
But once I realized it, these were places where I did not need to be.
I am anxiously waiting for God to sign me up…
To render a service in His Holy Church!
In His presence where I long to be
Ready, willing, and able, you will see!
When the appointment came, I accepted
To work, serve, and minister as requested.
And now I am content as I can be
To play a vital part in God's fa-mi-ly!
In a man's world, this place! And that place!
May not be the best!
And, as you know,
There is hardly any rest!
This one thing is assured to be!

In HIS KINGDOM, THERE IS A PLACE FOR ME!

## THE BUD
## (BITTERSWEET FLOWER)

Just like the bud is the prelude (development) to a flower, the prenatal period is the prelude to birthing a baby. Likewise, ordained purpose (i.e., spiritual gifts, talents, skills, creativity) is the prelude to divine destiny. Divine destiny is the spiritual landing place orchestrated by God—only when mankind pursues God's will, with passion, and walk according to His purpose.

I was born and reared in a small South Georgia town where varieties of beautiful azalea flowers individually arrayed in a rainbow of colors populated the landscape and postmarked the complexion of the city and community. On a weekend home visit, spiritual and sensitive collaboration with my parents (deceased) remained at an all-time high. On that documented day, the sun's rays triggered thermostat readings of over ninety degrees, therewith forcing a deficit of cool breeze. Nevertheless, the smell of flowers was in the air and birds were singing everywhere.

Revisiting and recollecting the biological genesis of my journey, on a cold/rainy winter's (Monday) morning, with the time clock of life ticking in my mother's womb, the time of delivery was at hand. From the onset, there was an array of anticipation and excitement. Then, the eclipse! A dark cloud of mortality throned the genesis of my birth to rob me from taking my place in society. The adversary was determined to take the limelight from the occasion. As history records, the process of giving birth presented an austere situation that the sought-after mid-wife was incapable of handling. Realizing the complexity of this long-awaited birth, Daddy was directed to seek professional/medical assistance at the local hospital.

According to further accounts concerning this incredible birth and the outlying factors involved, while Daddy raced through city streets (transporting Mom), honking the horn, defying red lights, stop signs, bushy tailed animals, and assorted vehicles to meet his greatest challenge, simultaneously, heart-wrenching emotions flowed through Daddy's veins. As a believer and standing on God's Word stilled his spirit. Upon arrival at the local hospital, the physical examination revealed that the delivery was even more complicated/challenging—the survival of both momma and baby was negative.

"I shall not die, but live, and declare the works of the Lord" (Psalm 118:17).

Time being of the essence, the doctor conceded to his limitations that the grave medical complications paralyzed his hand from saving both mother and child. In turn, Daddy was summoned with bittersweet news—the delivery would be very difficult, yet devastating; the doctor could only save one—mom or baby. To attempt to save both would be fatal. Daddy was asked the politically correct question, "Ward, which one do you want me to save?"

In a sarcastic manner, as Satan would have it mocking, ha! ha! ha! Who do you choose, Mr. Pitiful? On a more serious note, this was not up for debate, jawbone bashing, and certainly not funny. The ha! ha! ha! as the devil had planned (doomed and gloomed), was destined to be a ha-lle-lu-jah! as God had ordained in my mother's womb.

> "I knew you before I formed you in your mother's womb. Before you were born, I set you apart and appointed you as my prophet to the nations" (Jeremiah 1:5, NLT).

**Disclosure: "Not asserting to be a prophetess."**
**The Flower**

As a believer and spirit-led, Daddy indicated instantly (by confirmation) in his spirit that it was not the doctor's hand (expertise) that would save; it was going to take the Hand of God. Giving the doctor marching orders, Daddy responded, "I have six other children. If you cannot save but one, save my wife." Daddy, being a great man of faith and integrity, stood on the Word of God (never doubting) and declared that God's Word would not return unto Him void. Daddy believed and trusted God that mom and baby would be saved. The time clock tick-tocked, tick-tocked, and the clock hands turned second by second, minute by minute. The bud, bitter, yes, but thanks be to God, the sweet flower/baby girl inhaled her first breath outside her mother's womb, as destiny's child. Because *purpose* said hello to *destiny*, tailored-fitted in purposeful traveling shoes on her mission walk in Discovering Her Place, as a Bittersweet Flower. Daddy Ward oftentimes quoted (like the old adage), "The bud will have a bitter taste, sweeter would be the flower."

> To appoint unto them that mourn in Zion, to give unto them beauty for ashes, the oil of joy for mourning, the garment of praise for the spirit of heaviness; that they might be called trees of righteousness, the planting of the LORD, that he might be glorified.
> 
> Isaiah 61:3

**Take Away**

The bittersweet plant/flower has devastating characteristics as well. Invasive species, left unregulated, grow wildly out of control. "Bittersweet vines will literally take over the landscape, smothering out native species of trees, shrubs, and plantings. The tangled vines can also become so heavy that entire trees and plants may be uprooted once the bittersweet plant takes over."[6] It was Satan's desire to invade (take over) my mother's womb by ensnaring the birthing process, smothering out Mom's and baby's lives by grave (counterfeit) symptoms to cause fatal results.

The Blood of Jesus intervened by flowing through the umbilical cord, giving fresh breath/oxygen to both mother and child. All Glory be to God! The Holy Spirit strengthened the birthing process so organs, arteries, veins, blood vessels, etc. would not be punctured or uprooted by the bittersweet vine of devastation. Satan's malicious doomsday plot backfired. Incredibly, this triumphed as a glorious day with the SON. (Not the doctor that delivered me; it was like Daddy said, "The Mighty Hand of God.")

## PLACE OF DISCOVERY
## (NEW LOVE, MISSION, AND CLARION CALL)

Over the years, my decision was to journey in pursuit of moving forward spiritually (accepting Christ as Savior and Lord); however, I was not anticipating an immediate order to change partners. This would occur at an unexpected time. Meaning… Several years ago, my sole intention was to attend church revival and have an uplifting time and return home with no deliberate commitment to readjust my carnal path. Little did I know that it was my appointed time. When the revivalist asked me, "Do you believe that God can save you?" With such conviction, I responded, "I know God can save me!" Precisely, at that very moment, I was intellectually persuaded, coupled with a spiritual awakening (mindset changed) that befell. Sincerely, the mere essence of a teardrop of faith stampeded heaven evoking Divine Intervention into my presence. That permeation of Agape Love initiated spiritual transformation, unveiling my new love. The indelible love of God lifted me into an essential saintly place. My new love, as mystic in the natural as it seemed, was as awesome as HE in the spiritual; no one and not anything can compare to the Love of God.

As my journey became illuminated with the SON shining in my heart, I was contemplating the *what* and *what if* factors concerning enormous challenges and possibilities placed not only before me, but others as well. Majestically in the weakest hour, my heart tittered on the edge of night to imagine imminent victory on the eve of the break of day. With morning time nearing, I said, "Awake, awake, good morning, Holy Spirit!" Cascading emotions and draining pressures were overcome with the Hope of Glory! Therewith enlightening my inner soul with vision, joy, and tranquility to journey onward to realize My Purpose.

> "Lift up your heads, O ye gates; and be ye lift up, ye everlasting doors; and the King of glory shall come in" (Psalm 24:7).

The exodus from carnality (the bud) to the spiritual realm (new convert/the flower) is an enduring process destined to ignite uncomfortable emotions of relevance (i.e., tangible losses in relationships, loneliness, and oftentimes rejection). Satan's method of operation is working through individuals. Opposers may be family members, love connections, friends, and/or colleagues/cohorts because of the new walk. Rejected by those whom you think not may cause incredible loneliness. And with that reality, I was subject to experience a world of distance from normality as was once known.

Moreover, as time passed, the prevailing Spirit of God took precedence, providing restoration and preservation for my mind, soul, spirit, and body. Please know that the moment spiritual conception is activated (regenerating mindset), one can no longer be held hostage (spiritual enslavement) to carnal temptations that incite pressures and the captivity of Satan's chains. Subsequently, a journey of new life began in me.

> "Thou wilt keep *him* in perfect peace, *whose* mind *is* stayed *on thee*: because he trusteth in thee" (Isaiah 26:3).

I attempted to be very careful by tiptoeing through valley lows pertaining to the intricacies of life. However, my spirit was willing but my flesh was weak. To guard my heart, I became intentional by keeping a faith-filled mindset and my behavior positive. Besides, being saddled with tests and biased rejections, through it all with heart-drenching determination, my resolve was reinforced. Nevertheless, the glorious radiant hope of the WORD within enlightened my spirit, soothed my heart, reminding that the footsteps in the dusty sand are not mine, but God's! That, my friend, is when HE was carrying me. As time passed, as a chosen vessel, I accepted my call into the ministry. Staying focused on my heavenly calling allowed me to Discover My Place, My Purpose, and My Time to Propel.

## DIVINE PLACE OF DISCOVERY AS A BITTERSWEET FLOWER

In all walks of life (i.e., social, religious, political, public/private industries, etc.), Satan's plan is to abort ambition while deflating dreams; suspend spiritual gifts and make us comfortable with procrastination; terminate talents by simply walking away; cripple creativity to smother out what is and the greater me/you (within) that could possibly be. All in all, behaving as if man's destiny is a figment of the imagination, irrelevant to principle, preparation, and providence. If not careful, the overwhelming molestation of positive emotions, the prostitute of loneliness, and the rejection and regret will culminate into an avalanche of despair, evoking a silent storm within one's spirit. Notwithstanding, while experiencing the law of diminishing return, and unable to extricate the tempest of temptation that threatens the straight path and the preeminent place, climaxing with distractions and detours designed to hinder the purpose and promises of God.

The predestined will of man is to choose his/her path (good or evil); abundant life over death robs Satan of his perspective victory to steal, kill, and destroy mankind. By choosing God's way, the prepossessing pessimistic spirit that wars against the flesh vanishes due to the innate love and God-given power within, which is the Holy Spirit, reassuring us that the safest place is in the Will of God.

"The thief cometh not, but to steal and to kill and to destroy: I am come that they might have life, and that they might have it more abundantly" (John 10:10).

## POEM:
## "COLOR ME RAINBOW"

There is a rainbow in the sky
Sent from heaven from on high.
See the beauty as it adorns,
Draped in colorful fashion; meticulously formed.

Rainbow symbolizes New Beginnings
Prompting to put away dark endings.
It is the daylight of today
starting new life in the cool of the day.
Take hold of your rainbow in your heart
that will give you a fresh start.

To experience the glory of all
When counting God's blessings, large or small.
The rainbow is real
and waiting for you to feel
the love, passion that is buried inside to be revealed.

So, excavate the rainbow treasure
that lives within
to produce radiant glory to comprehend.
When writing a new song of praise;

Thus
a new story to embrace; moving forward in new ways.

Look up and admire the vibrant colors
Clothed in Majesty, none like no other.

God sent a message long ago
by way of a Colorful Rainbow
Thus
the Bible tells me so.
The earth will not be destroyed
by flood anymore.

Unfortunately, man continued to disobey
While sin took main stage.
Man refused to repent;
rather, folly, drink and dine
God promised no more water but fire next time.

God put the rainbow in the sky
"New Beginnings"
If we try—
and know that HIS love will never die.

## SAFELY IN HIS ARMS
## (Spiritual Confirmation)

In the twilight of daybreak (the bud), while slumbering in my sleep, half-conscious in a visionary state of mind, the enemy/adversary was in hot pursuit of my very being. The figurative midnight journey commenced at the place (homestead) where I grew up. It was in the quaint community known as "Lil Miami" where peach cobbler and homemade ice cream were a southern/Sunday delight. Culminating the family gathering, hugs, kisses, and departing phrases such as "love you" and "so long, see you later" were as common as a drink of water. Suddenly a depiction of a giant monster (evil spirit) called out and targeted my spouse, Neal, and I. Thereto, the deadly pursuit, abstract of destruction (physical/spiritual) was on.

> The Lord is my light and my salvation; whom shall, I fear? The Lord is the strength of my life; of whom shall I be afraid? When the wicked even my enemies and my foes, came upon me to eat up my flesh, they stumbled and fell.
>
> Psalm 27:1–2

As we vigorously journeyed across the thicket (depicted as natural/spiritual landscape), the thistles and thorns (of life), marched in muddy waters (i.e., injustice, rejection, human frailty), and jumped across hurdles and obstacles, the swamp-infested area (tests, trials) resisted vehemently to relinquish her degrading terrain (situations). The journey was hectic and weariness displayed its ugly head along the way, but there was no turning back. The enemy seemed close, but he could not overtake or destroy. Running hand-in-hand and with eyes fixed on the "lighthouse" (stationed on a hill that seemed so far away) that guided our every stride. Divine empowerment propelled our inner determination to sit in the presence of that true light. In all its glory, the lighthouse reigned on top of the mountain with ordered steps/platforms of design and challenges to conquer and defeat prior to going to the next level, ultimately reaching the summit.

> "When Jesus spoke again to the people, he said, 'I am the light of the world. Whosoever follows me will never walk-in darkness, but will have the light of life'" (John 8:12, NIV).

While under tumultuous circumstances, the quest was challenging, but our eyes fixed on "that place." Howbeit arriving at the foot of the mountain revealed levels of progression depicting horizontal platforms surrounding the mountain, each level higher than the other. Metaphorically, each platform portrayed laborers of various craftsmanship (i.e., weaving, knitting, carpentry, painting, etc.). Professionals and clergy, along with white collar/blue-collar workers: teaching, preaching, and assisting others in every aspect of their endeavor. Also, utilizing strategic resources; working with their hands utilizing technology, tools, and machinery. Each one represented their gifts, talents and skill set and purpose.

> "Every good gift and every perfect gift is from above, and comes down from the Father of lights, with whom is no variation or shadow of turning" (James 1:17, NKJV).

Considering the levels (good, bad, and ugly) involved in pursuing one's destiny, brings to mind an old Negro spiritual, "We Are Climbing Jacob's Ladder." Years ago, while under the tutelage of my parents, Momma Mearlon would rise early in the morning preparing breakfast for the family. Cuddling my pillow a little longer was no threat to the aroma of homemade buttermilk biscuits infiltrating the atmosphere and enjoying the succulent taste on my palate. Siblings, Elaine, Louvenia, Mattie, Margie, David, and Ann were also delighted to get up and enjoy the southern-style breakfast with all its trimmings. They would concur, Momma would rise early in the morning singing the old Negro spiritual:

> Rise, shine, give God (the) Glory,
> (Repeat 3 times)
> Soldiers of the Cross.
>
> We are climbing Jacob's Ladder,
> (Repeat 3 times)
> Soldiers of the Cross.
>
> Every round goes higher, higher,
> (Repeat 3 times)
> Soldiers of the Cross.
>
> Do you think I'd make a soldier?
> (Repeat 3 times)
> Soldiers of the Cross.

Truly, Momma Mearlon was a virtuous woman. The lyrics, "every round goes higher, higher" reminds me of how the platforms were constructed from bottom to top. Each had advanced levels to conquer, such as life, prior to proceeding to the next level—in pursuit of divine destiny. The quest in reaching the lighthouse was a courageous effort to subdue each platform that provoked a new level of experience. Also, there was pre-determined work to be performed successfully prior to going to the next level.

"Do not demise these small beginnings, for the LORD rejoices to see the work begin, to see the plumb line in Zerubbabel's hand" (Zechariah 4:10, NLT).

As such, the lighthouse (the flower) represented safety (from the enemy); peace (that surpasses all understanding), and rest (from our labor). When the last level on this mountain was reached and all work was completed, the Glory of God filled the room with an immaculate light that the human eye was unable to behold. I was miraculously swooped into the star-bright place without need of walking through the opened door or climbing into opened windows. The Hand of God lifted me!

"Send out your light and your truth; let them lead me; let them bring me to your holy hill and to your dwelling!" (Psalm 43:3, ESV).

The SON shined, and celestial elements framed the doorway and infiltrated the window seals. Being immersed with all the glory; here thereto, the consciousness of mind sensed the absence of my significant other beside me. In a twinkling of an eye, the same radiant force/power swooped Neal in beside me. We were vivaciously declaring, "Oh, what peace, joy, and contentment filled the place" as we were engrossed with the

Glory of God. Triumphantly declaring that we were "safely in His arms."

> Now, I have discovered my place of rest,
> and no other place is the best.
> That place is political and is figurative;
> this place is factual and is spiritual.
> That place is dangerous, with lots of unrest;
> now I can relax in His Holiness.

Staying focused on divine destiny and eyes fastened on the lighthouse will guide you in Discovering Your Place.

## POEM:
## "U-2"

As I travel from me to you, our roads are similar
whether black or blue.
Reflecting on what was, what is, and what can be
U-2 is vulnerable as me.

Dark clouds of life are eminent in everyone's lives
Faith, hope, and love are radiant as the blue skies.

On your journey you will encounter bittersweet times
Do not give up and give in to artificial beginnings
and futile endings.

Various hurts we all endured, many a toxic battle
Oftentimes misunderstood.
As time passes, this will be at last
U-2 shall know, and Me-2, that this too shall pass.

The straight path is the route to promising victory
When you gird up in truth, put on gospel shoes
and embrace the Good News.

Keep traveling onward to the upward way
Staying focused and preserved day-by-day.

As you become established and settled in Psalms of
Hymns and Me-lo-dy
God's Word and wisdom are most tellingly.

Sing and rejoice as you take your stance
Steadfast and unmovable is the glorious plan.
Stand up, look up, in awe, heavenly
as you thrive and strive toward divine destiny.

CHAPTER 2

# Your World—Discovering Your Place

## INVESTIGATIVE DISCOVERY

Where are you? This is the same rhetorical question that our Lord God posed to Adam while in the Garden of Eden. "And the Lord God called to Adam, and said unto him, Where art thou?" (Genesis 3:9). Not that God did not know the answer, but was permitting Adam to consider a) Spiritual Place/Mindset (divine charge/accountability), and b) Physical Place/Hiding Site (nakedness/shame; responsibility) prior to responding. Adam's physical place is substantially entwined with his spiritual place of worship with God. Unfortunately, Adam's physical/hiding place became a spiritual cave walloping in a bitter blanket of darkness, void of sacred rest because of disobedience.

Likewise, the question remains open to cause a reckoning within humanity's intellectual, physical, and spiritual place. Twenty-first century Adam and culturally modern-day Eve, where are you intellectually (mentally/choices), spiritually (divinely, piously, resolve), and physically (bodily, environment) while traveling on life's journey? Take a break and reflect momentarily on this question. Now, what is your resolve?

This trail of investigative discovery more often than not leads to winding roads that enter into your world; a world filled with assorted experiences. What about happy times and sad days? Or public commendations, personal achievements, even some unspoken failures? A little here and a little there believing that the here and there are no more than the span of time allotted while en route to destiny.

In the natural setting, when a crime is committed, the onset of the investigation launches with securing the crime scene, interviewing witnesses (if any), and searching for evidence and motive. In comprehension of the intricate and moving parts surrounding the investigation, the crime scene is secured to minimize tampering. Therewith, eyewitnesses (first-hand accounts), evidence (facts), and motives are pivotal in solving the crime and tenaciously brought to the forefront. Oops, before we can move on, "Is there any person(s) of interest?" Oh yes. You.

Hence, as the journey of humanity embroils into a lengthy trip of self-discovery, misconduct is evaluated by considerable motives. For example: inalienable rights vs. imposed rights; poor/mediocrity vs. standard/excellent performance; accountability vs. irresponsibility; dependability vs. unreliability; transparent vs. obscure behavior; good vs. bad; success vs. failure; your way vs. God's way. As evidence is compiled, the scene is secured with spiritual confirmation that initiates relentless thought-provoking questions that arouse and captivate the hostage mind. Questions such as: a) Where is My place, b) What is My purpose and, c) When is My time to propel/pursue? Wherein hereafter referenced as the (3-WP's). These questions serve a two-fold purpose: 1) To ponder the inner man (spirit), and 2) To serve as a security screen to block out and eliminate flagrant noise from eroding your thought process.

> "The Lord is the portion of mine inheritance and of my cup: thou maintainest my lot. The lines are fallen unto me in pleasant places; yea, I have a goodly, heritage" (Psalm 16:5–6).

Subsequently, in the search stage, there is no prospect of surrender until all issues of life are reckoned with, acknowledged, forgiven, and restored. You must be willing to embrace these pertinent questions to evaluate your motives, actions, and prospective outcomes in every concern. The *what* of the matter is interwoven into the *where*. Somewhere, but where? Predicated on sound decisions, the path one chooses and the steps one takes will ultimately lead to a cherubic rainbow, where skies are blue: purpose.

> "Beloved, I wish above all things that thou mayest prosper and be in health, even as thy soul prospereth" (3 John 1:2).

*Where* is a hard spot that drives motive for assessing and determining destination and/or point of contact—be it carnal or spiritual. You truly do not know where you are going until you comprehend where you are. Impromptu decisions, premature action, and irresponsible willpower climaxes to "no-where land," thusly, finding oneself in a desert-dry, weary, and unproductive land where no cooling water flow.

Decisiveness is defined: "the characteristic or practice of deciding or acting without hesitation; resoluteness."[7] Conversely, indecisiveness is defined as: "hesitating, uncertain, wavering, doubtful, faltering..." etc.[8] Wrestling with indecisiveness is one primary tool the enemy employs to provoke doubt. And in the battle of doubt, rational decisions scarcely exist. Wavering thoughts lead to unstable actions proven to be unsuccessful in moving forward in a consistent manner. Mind you, whatever decisions (spiritual or carnal) are needed to perform in this cycle of life, the decisions must be sound to benefit the whole person. In the event change does not occur, this conflicting behavior will eventually leave you stagnant with apprehension/trepidation.

"A double minded man is unstable in all his ways" (James 1:8).

Upon reaching the thought-provoking decision in choosing the right path, thereby prompting an affirmative stance, the conclusion of the matter is consummated in a divine passion that propels favorable outcome. By making the right choice with this, my friend, the optimal move has begun in your vessel. The stimulus to *what* and *where* is *when*. *When* is circumference within a designated, appointed time-period. Brother/sister, now is your time to travel a little farther down discovery lane, known as 3-WP's. (Where is My Place? What is My Purpose? When is My time to Propel/Pursue?)

"To everything there is a season, and a time to every purpose under the heaven" (Ecclesiastes 3:1).

"I said in mine heart, God shall judge the righteous and the wicked: for there is a time there for every purpose and for every work" (Ecclesiastes 3:17).

## WHERE IS MY PLACE?

Glad you asked. *Place* has a two-fold meaning:

**First (Spiritual Place/Mindset)**
Sacred place: The tabernacle inside one's soul is a divine vacuum that God created and only HE can fill. Further elaboration entails as referenced: "A paraphrase of Blaise Pascal's work goes like this, 'There is a God-shaped vacuum in the heart of every person which cannot be filled by any created thing, but only by God the Creator, made known through Jesus Christ.'"[9]

People, places, and things will always leave something to be desired, thereby being incapable of fulfilling this divine cavity. This predestined place is the bedrock of purpose. Regardless of where you go (secular), you will never find another place that is so sacred and sweet. A place of serenity and unconditional love that only God can give. In the quietness of one's spirit, at some point in time, every human being has the ability to discern the love of God as Creator, and has a spiritual bond constituting spiritual awareness. This divine channel is a place of peace and a reservoir of spiritual enlightenment (moral consciousness) to guide and nourish the God-given purpose to excavate within.

Man's soulish aspect incorporates intellect, feelings, emotions inclusive of volition power. Functioning together, the mind is where cerebral reckoning begins (thought process); decisions are made to choose right or wrong. The question becomes, "Am I mentally opened to hear from God?" Whatever decision is made will determine one's course of action in living a blessed life (choosing good) as opposed to living a defeated life (choosing evil). We must be willing to rid our minds of selfish desires and fleeting expectations and turn to God for His plan for our life. (Change begins in the mind.)

> The human race was created by God with spirit, soul, and body. The "inner man" is another way of describing the spiritual aspect of a person. The "outer man," by contrast, would be the visible, external aspect of a person.[10]

> The soul is the spiritual nature of humankind. It is the incorporeal essence of humankind, and it is thought to be separable from the body at death. In life, it is credited with the faculties of thought, action, and emotion. The mind is man's faculty of thinking, reasoning, and applying knowledge. It is human consciousness that starts in the brain and is manifested through man's thoughts, actions, emotion, will, memory, and imagination.[11]

"And the very God of peace sanctify you wholly; and I pray God your whole spirit and soul and body be preserved blameless unto the coming of our Lord Jesus Christ" (1 Thessalonians 5:23).

Divine place matures in the heart of the mind (meditate) where decisions are made to obey or disobey. As the soul (will) of man desires to do good, his/her spirit communes with God, cultivating into thoughts, decisions, and subsequent actions that ignite divine awareness, culminating into positive resolve. As you consistently walk and demonstrate this affirmative behavior, it transcends into pious character that will facilitate making better choices on life's journey. Even more so, it is to ensure a safe destiny landing.

> This book of the law shall not depart out of thy mouth; but thou shalt meditate therein day and night, that thou mayest observe to do according to all that is written therein: for then shou shalt make thy way prosperous, and then thou shalt have good success.
>
> Joshua 1:8

On the other hand, as your soul desires to do good, the adversary is there to intercept the spiritual connection with God. This is initiated by causing varied negative thoughts, lies, and doubt to yield a bad decision. Yet you must also understand that contrary choices lead to a bitter blanket of spiritual nakedness; a midnight of misconstrued revelation and subordinate consecration to be deliberated upon. Without devoted execution, we will lie blemished on life's pathway.

> "You make known to me the path of life; in your presence there is fullness of joy; at your right hand are pleasures forevermore" (Psalm 16:11, ESV).

Whatever deed (good, bad, or indifferent) starts with our intellect (mind). If thoughts prevail long enough, entertainment of implementation is foremost. Aside, to grasp your mission, passion, and purpose, it must be settled first in your mind. So, when intellectually realized, a place of evaluation can commence by determining whether you are in a good place. That place is where passion, gift (seed) can be watered and nurtured into fruition. Remember, if you are out of place, your purpose will be impeded and unperfected. *Divine place is where ordained purpose is nourished, germinating into execution.*

Reading the scriptures reflected in Exodus 3:1–5, 9–12 reveal God's clarion call to Moses to lead the children of Israel out of Egypt (bondage). For Moses to be productive required: 1) Open mindset—attentive to

God, and 2) Wholesome environment to commune effectively with God.

As Moses "led the flock to the backside of the desert and came to the mountain of God, even to Horeb, and the angel of the Lord appeared to him in a flame of fire out of the midst of a burning bush," Moses was intrigued by the unconsumable burning bush. As Moses attempted to observe closer, God called to him (out of the midst of the burning bush), commanding: a) Not to come any closer, and b) Take off his shoes from his feet. Accordingly, God announced: the place where Moses stood was Holy Ground. Through this directive, the Lord got Moses' attention to: a) focus and hear from God, b) embrace a consecrated/peaceful spirit (innerman), and c) realize the value of a wholesome environment to receive divine assignment/mission/purpose.

Furthermore, by safeguarding the overall process, Moses was prevented from being distracted by negativity and the compromising noise from the people that he left behind. As a result of being obedient, he ultimately fulfilled his purpose by leading the Children of Israel out of Egypt. Otherwise, contrary actions would have impeded his mission. There are times when you may have to leave some people behind in order to hear from God and carry out your mission established in your divine place.

"Have I not commanded you? Be strong and of good courage; do not be afraid, nor be dismayed for the Lord your God is with you wherever you go" (Joshua 1:9, NKJV).

**Secondly (Physical Place/Environment)**

State of quality: Wholesome settings versus unhealthy settings. Whether conducive and productive or detrimental and unfruitful are resulting measures that should be considered predicated on the types of environments chosen.

For further elaboration, in the spiritual realm, under God's direction, strive to walk by ordered steps. Saintly behavior must be prevalent as a devoted Christian. The prince of the world is Satan: the adversary/evil one. Essentially, for purpose to have a conducive place to thrive, detox your mind and get in a wholesome place to commune with God. When God speaks to your situation, be obedient to His will. Eliminate unfruitful (tangible and intangible) distractions such as noise (silent/disturbed spirit, or audible/loud, perceptible) that will help reduce cluttered minds. Additionally, eradicate unhealthy conversations, subjective nice/nasty interactions, and activities (across the board) that suffocate creativity and productivity, resulting in abolishing quality time that is unredeemable.

"Where no counsel is, the people fall: but in the multitude of counsellors there is safety" (Proverbs 11:14).

"Wherefore come out from among them, and be ye separate, saith the Lord, and touch not the unclean thing; and I will receive you" (2 Corinthians 6:17).

Unless spiritual detoxication takes place, sojourning in this realm can be likened to traveling the fast lane. Emphasizing this point, on the autobahn route in Germany, there is no federally mandated speed limit for some vehicles. Likewise, in the secular fast lane, social environments, orchestrated mainstreams, hidden agendas, and enticing masquerades are strategically planned where there is no set perimeter for intemperance. Why? Because it is designed to incite various settings of Pomp and Circumstance, at-will behavior, and controlled participation, resulting in disordered steps and spiritual unrest.

"The steps of a good man are ordered by the Lord: and he delighteth in his way" (Psalm 37:23).

Satan's aim is to hinder you from becoming what God has ordained. Rather, he would keep you chained and bound into the depths of disparity, depravity, and degradation. Besides, as believers have accepted Christ as Savior, by the redemptive blood of Jesus, we are no longer chained by our sin nature, but are restored and clothed in "robe of righteousness" as referenced in Isaiah 61:10. That said, when God looks on the believer, he sees the shed blood of Jesus (Holy covering) and not the sin nature of man. He only sees HIS goodness within.

Many places and establishments are redesigned to attract people of all walks of life. Some are depicted on large displays on scenic routes, interstate highways, city streets, and so forth, with people with smiling faces—advertisements, attractions, propaganda, etc. The culture of powerful men/women, and influential mentors of mainstream institutions, establishments (i.e., social, religious, political, public/private sector) easily fall prey to grandiose delusions attempting to dismiss any form of lesser significance.

In close circuit, truth discloses wired smiles displayed that produce short-circuit advancement, temporary return, and a bitter end. The charade highlights frowns of failed promises, hidden agendas equated to being abused and accursed—raped of self-esteem, self-worth, and trapped in adulterous affairs levying mind over matter. What is more, the pass-over of elevation/promotion is indicative of unwarranted rejection. Rejection for whatever reason becomes the main course served on your persona. At the same time, deeds of unfairness are displayed to diminish rather than honor the significant person. Why? Because the "seat" is "reserved" for a select few. This biased behavior barely hinges on the shadow of fairness and integrity. The humanity of morality and justification merely exist. So, as the need for a change agent arises, in the meantime, the who's who, movers and shakers, and wannabes paint their true color as a faded rose.

Evidence lies in the attractions of city life (night life, bright lights, glitter/gold, wine and roses, prestigious parties) designed for select socioeconomic classes of people. Wherewithal, in every aspect of life (absent of the in-crowd), the curious, men-pleasers long for an open door that appears to be golden, only to discover for "Members Only"—the elite, pride and prejudice, VIPs, the prestige and privilege. Oh well, no invite, no assignment or promotion. No camaraderie with persons of distinction. Wherefore, there are a myriad of activities to enjoy, opportunities of advancement, absence of your name. Has it occurred to you that you are out of place?

> No temptation has overtaken you except such as is common to man; but God is faithful, who will not allow you to be tempted beyond what you are able, but with the temptation will also make the way of escape, that you may be able to bear it.
>
> 1 Corinthians 10:13 (NKJV)

There again, howbeit, that masquerades of people frequent many places with an array of false credentials and insufficient funds to sustain them while on a one-way ticket to a wonderland of no return. Likened to a roller coaster in an amusement park, which is an "an elevated railway...constructed with sharp curves and steep inclines on which cars roll."[12] Doing things your way will keep you spending out of control with indefinite twists and turns, highs and lows. Exposed and living on the edge with immeasurable overturns. Please know that God has a better place and purpose for your life.

When out of place, you are unable to receive all that God has for you. Oh, you may get a trickle here and there, but your potential is limited, and your mission is shackled once again. Why? Because you are all over the place—not His place. Whereas, the ideal thing to do is to make room for Him. Be careful not to allow the bittersweet vine of destruction to uproot your dream, abandon your purpose, and disregard your divine destiny. The best possible effort will be to keep your place refined while walking out your soul salvation.

This predestined path in seeking one's place and purpose is individually designed. Oftentimes, it is a lonesome walk that will test the very essence of your stance. When Jesus' mission was at hand, His deliberate decision was to take three of His inner circle of disciples (Peter, James, and John) with Him to pray. Well, it turned out to be a soul-searching task. The disciples fell asleep, and it was incumbent upon Jesus to walk alone to find that hallowed place to pray. In that destined hour, Jesus turned His attention from the heart-rending cup that revealed His sacrificial assignment regarding His Crosswalk mission. A mission full of torture: restrained with chains, hammered with bangs, pangs, beaten with a whip (sixty-six bloody stripes on His back), piercing nails in His side/feet, silent groans, head of thorns—all culminating in His death on the cross. As Jesus entreated for the bitter cup to pass from Him; by searching His heart, He concluded, "Nevertheless not my will, but thine, be done" (Luke 22:42)). Humbly, Jesus looked to God, who is the Author and Finisher of Our Faith, and the glory that awaited him in fulfilling His Crosswalk.

Sometimes you must leave your company and steal away to hear from God. The providential place is a consecrated place where there is no physical interference with people, projects, pets, or press (social media). In answering the call/assignment/mission, we too must search our hearts, and be resolute when we say, "God, not my will, but Your will be done." The same grace will be afforded to all (as Jesus) when we do accordingly.

Do you remember the captivating tranquility when you discovered your place? If there is anyone who has not discovered your place, refer again to the providential place in this paragraph and begin your search.

What about Christian ministry? Yes, that too. But before we move on, it is important to define this subject. According to Wikipedia, "In Christianity, ministry is an activity carried out by Christians to express or spread their faith, the prototype being the Great Commission. The Encyclopedia of Christianity defines it as 'carrying forth Christ's mission in the world,' indicating that it is 'conferred on each Christian in baptism.'"[13]

By the same token, we can reason that many are out of place while serving in the household of faith. Nevertheless, they continue to function in denial—simply as a mere excuse to plot one's own course. And as long as believers function in this capacity, they prohibit their ordained purpose from coming into fruition.

> "The heart of man plans his way, but the Lord establishes his steps" (Proverbs 16:9, ESV).

Pause for a moment and consider: Are you traveling on the yellow brick road trying to find your way home like the character, Dorothy, in the *Wizard of Oz*? Oh, well. No time for identity crisis, uncertainty, or sob stories, like Dorothy. One foot in/one out; stay or go; yes or no. If the answer is yes, then turn off the night light (distractions, doubt, and despair) and turn on the morning star (hope, health, and happiness). You are now ready to put on the golden slippers to march onto the Road of Zion, the spiritual landscape route. At the junction, yielding right, the streets are paved with gold, the pathway that leads to abundant life. Morning glory is just over the horizon. Apart from that, trekking the secular route (yellow-brick road) yielding left of the junction, is the broad murky road that leads to destruction.

> "Set your affection on things above, not on things on the earth" (Colossians 3:2).

As the quest continues, look ahead. What do you see? What is your vision, goal, and mission wrapped in the envelope of life? Considering the spiritual realm, and for practical purposes in harmony with this manuscript, to be nearsighted is to see self; self-centeredness (my way—temporal). Otherwise, to be farsighted is to see God afar off; (God way/spiritual). Is your vision, goal, or mission self-centered or God-centered? Look closely with assurance and turn right, a spiritually opened door full of life, liberty, and the joy of the Lord in Christ Jesus is at hand. Why not transform selfishness into a spiritual song? Seize the moment and secure a physical environment that will endorse the Kingdom of God.

"**There** is a way which seemeth **right** unto a man, but the end thereof are the ways of death" **(Proverbs 14:12).**

**(The Bud—Bitter)**

Biblical scripture (Luke 15:11–32) teaches of a prodigal son born into a wealthy family who, over time, asked his father for his portion of the inheritance. He desired to be in the in-crowd; fast lane. The prodigal son received his portion, left home, and journeyed to a foreign country where he spent all of his inheritance on riotous living. Final analysis: he left on high status—ended up on hog pen status. Unfortunately, he was poverty-stricken, resulting in dreadful want that harshly facilitated the moment of truth. The prodigal son came to himself and realized who he was and not what he looked or smelled like! Clothed with a penitent spirit and contrite heart, he rediscovered his place—that place called home. His humble intent was nothing greater than to return as a servant.

**(The Flower—Sweet)**

But while walking barefoot on the dirty, dusty road home, his father saw him from a distance and met him. Displaying genuine love, his father kissed him and provided the best robe, endorsing his return. A ring was placed on his hand, representative of power. Revealing another element of the prominent attire, the father placed sandals on his feet to certify his place as a son, not a servant. The planned celebration included pomp and circumstance that commenced honoring his return home.

**(The Bud—Bitter)**

Likewise, in our modern culture, the prodigal masquerader (male/female) finds themselves in the wrong place, a foreign land (i.e., physically, spiritually, emotionally, intellectually), with no sense of direction and a false expectancy that cannot be fulfilled that reaches farther than the eye can behold. Nevertheless, stripped of God-given talent and having abandoned their gifts, this results in a trip of nakedness, desolation, and devastation. Emotionally torn in pieces, ripped in humiliation and despair, with a seared cloud of doubt hovering over that annihilates self-value, dignity, and wholesomeness, which now is a thing of the past. The weight of sin carries an odor in the nostrils of humanity that only the Blood of Jesus can sanitize.

> "These people draw near to Me with their mouth, and honor Me with their lips, but their heart is far from Me" (Matthew 15:8, NKJV).

**(The Flower—Sweet)**

As man is created in the image of God, the void that man experiences when separated from Him is longing for the *agape* love of God. This love transcends our inner being, the homeland of the soul. Apart from that, the hollowness cannot be filled. Only when mankind returns back to God, in harmony (fellowship and relationship), will he/she be at home and made whole. As the scripture reference in the story of the prodigal son states, "And when he came to himself..." Prior to that statement, the prodigal son never made any positive adjustments until his mindset was truly changed. He reassessed his situation, pondered the blessings he left behind, and took positive action to rediscover his place. Likewise, you must come to yourself (change of heart/mindset), which is predicated on discovering your divine place—subsequently positive actions will follow. This will happen when you reconsider where you are. If caught on a wilderness journey, allow prayer to decimate the faithless forest in order to see the Tree of Life and walk out in victory. *Remember, the choices made in life serve as forerunners that determine one's destiny.*

A spiritual mindset endorses prudent decisions that will cultivate a wholesome physical environment needed to fulfill your purpose. This must be your primary focal point and spiritual delight while traveling on the road to divine destiny. Contrarily, oftentimes many attempts to walk in the divine place are unconducive for purpose to be effectively fulfilled. This is due to having let down your guard. Whereby a carnal mindset instigates questionable environments inclusive of people, associations, music, TV, social media—to name a few—causing spiritual contamination. In so doing, our social and physical environment becomes spiritually raped of the excellence that it can give. As a result, the fragrance of the anointing dissipates. And in many instances, it is delayed but not denied when your focus is reevaluated for positive change. This is a good time to regroup and reassess your environment by spiritually sweeping the road you are traveling to tap into your purpose for a rewarding outcome. Look beyond what you see and embrace what is revealed.

## POEM:
## "REFLECTIONS"

Look in the mirror and see clearly
reflections on the other side
are you, my dearly?

Look at self, do not be afraid
Is it inviting or a dread?
What do you see?
Reflection of life staring back at me.

Reflections in the mirror, this I see.
Wondering, in fact, is this truly me?
I see a person drifting from standing tall
aborting God's favor and glorious call.

Stop the bull and prepare for divine renewal
Benediction of the past
opting for a restoration that will last.

Not too late, so make a date
to meet the Savior at the Gate.
Who will welcome you in as a friend,
and stay true to you through journey's end.

God has purpose for your life
waiting for you to realize.
When you discover your
treasure chest of gift(s) within,
Glory be to God, you will win.

Stay consecrated and reveal
that the gift of God is the real deal.
Your gift is sacred for you to use;
bless others and not misuse.

This is a blessing from on high
that no one can deny.
Fresh anointing, the fountain of praise;
giving off light and everyone can engage.
Praise the Father and the Son
New found favor has begun.
To harness, hone, and make known
God's glorious work—
Reflections of the Master have begun.
Now, when I look in the mirror
What do I see?
Reflections of the Master
Looking back at me.

## WHAT IS MY PURPOSE?

> "For I know the plans I have for you, declares the Lord, plans to prosper you and not to harm you, plans to give you hope and a future" (Jeremiah 29:11, NIV).

There is God-given purpose in every human being.. *Britannica Dictionary*: "The reason why something is done or used: the aim or intention of something."[14] More importantly, the Sovereign God of all creation, the giver of life, and master of the universe created man for his glory and ultimately to glorify him.

> "Being predestinated according to the purpose of him who worketh all things after the counsel of his own will" (Ephesians 1:11).

> "Fear God, and keep his commandments: for this is the whole duty of man. For God shall bring every work into judgement, with every secret thing, whether it be good, or whether it be evil" (Ecclesiastes 12:13–14).

What is predestination?... The words translated "predestined" in the Scriptures...are from the Greek word *proorizo*, which carries the meaning of "determining beforehand," "ordaining," "deciding ahead of time."

So, predestination is God determining certain things to occur ahead of time.[15]

Being enthralled with the God-given passion within, there is no rest in the spirit until the "IT" factor (i.e., gifts, talents, skills, creativity) is acknowledged, activated, and fulfilled. For that cause, ask God for guidance and you will have found your purpose. As mentioned earlier, conceptualizing destiny is the perpetual landing place of purpose; tailored and orchestrated by God. Reference, *King James Dictionary*: "Purpose always includes the end in view."[16]

"And we know that all things work together for good to them that love God, to them who are the called according to his purpose" (Romans 8:28).

From the moment God created man, purpose was designed as part of humanity's fingerprint, i.e., DNA/ Divine Nature Aroma. Because everyone is unique, every person has a different fingerprint and specific "something" that he/she is designed to do, develop, and achieve by way of distinctive qualities (potentials, abilities, talents) that are divinely called or chosen. What is in your hand? What talent, gift, skill set, or creative measure lies dormant, deterring you from captivating, utilizing, and capitalizing for Kingdom purpose?

Failing to walk in divine purpose, the adversary of slothfulness, procrastination, doubt, trepidation, or other hinderances has crippled your progress in moving diligently toward your divine destiny. Purpose germinates and thrives in a divine place that is in order. Also, where wisdom prevails is destined to finish the course in a deliberate manner. What on earth is preventing you from answering the call? Mull this over—then get up and get going! Contrariwise, if spiritually contaminated, in many instances, the end result will be:

 a) doing something you were not destined to do (substitute plan);
 b) allowing others to push you into an unproductive mission (man's influence);
 c) not hearing from God; doing what carnality dictates (self-serving); and
 d) doing something simply because someone else is doing it (covetous matter).

As such, many are caused to abort their true purpose and identity. In many instances, "good work" is accomplished, but still remains outside the will of God for your life. (Yes, you can be doing good things, but not what God ordained). This is why it is imperative to discover your divine place to fully develop spiritually.

In order for your purpose to be fruitful, first seek your wholesome place for productive development, and in that way, the greatness in you shall be revealed.

While everyone has a purpose, many do not realize and know what it is. Nevertheless, there are those who realize and identify with it but are swayed not to pursue it due to an assortment of internal and external pressures, echoing Satan's lies. Pressures that leave one naked—suffocating with insecurity; trepidation, and procrastination, with a myriad of toxic statements toward oneself such as *Just who am I? What do I have to offer compared to others?* Further, asserting: *I'm not good enough; not qualified; not saved; they will never accept me,* and the self-assaults go on. Stop! Help is on the way. God's desire is that humanity thrives by living a blessed life. To live life without hope and purpose is likened to a bubble waiting indefinitely to burst. Hope gives confidence to wish upon a star; the Morning Star. That is, Jesus, and expect to have an abundant life and an expected end.

Do you understand that purpose is a deep moving unction (passion) within that stirs the soul? It will not rest until fruition is reached. However, this passion will only lie dormant for a season. When the season has expired, the vessel in which it was given ceases to reach his/her full potential due to unproductivity, without zeal, etc. Consequently, God-given passion is dried up and abandoned in the valley of dry bones, where spiritual hydration is desolate.

In the valley of dry bones, there is no value to the method of madness that exists in this spiritual desert where prudent factors are diminished and the conscious mind is seared. Everything is dead, spiritually cold and calculating. Moreover, you live as a ship without a sail floating along grasping for wind/breath. Every inch of the mile seems farther and farther away with no rest in sight. (Attempting to search for what you had all the time.) So, one keeps on sailing until the day darkens, realizing there is no real horizon; only a myth as the ship of life docks without a tugboat to pull her in. Relative to the vessel, purpose momentarily escapes her destiny only until the vessel rediscovers his/her place; and ultimately return to resolve the incredible journey to home. You will not be able to realize your purpose until you truly discover or refine your place.

> "A merry heart doeth good like a medicine: but a broken spirit drieth the bones" (Proverbs 17:22).

How do you tap into this divine place of discovery? First, it is a mindset sanctioned by God. A renewed mind is to be immersed in peace and empowered in liberty with spiritual resolve. This process encompasses intellectual reckoning that is entwined with undefeatable faith and agape love that transcends the end of time.

"Let this mind be in you, which was also in Christ Jesus" **(Philippians 2:5)**.

You must come to God willingly to tap into your place and consummate the journey while walking in your divine purpose. The repentant individual must come in spirit and in truth—boldly before the throne of grace to have ultimate victory in Christ Jesus. The believer is also summoned to exercise the prayer below, asking God to forgive all transgressions (complete transparency), because during the course of a day, "little foxes" (shortcomings) may have displayed their ugly head. Little foxes can hinder close circuit communication to hear from God. If procrastination or any other hindrances have caused a setback, now is the time to renew your commitment and drive to fulfill the mission that God has set before you. Nevertheless, hindrances may also serve as a decoy to terminate your true desire in discovering your divine place to live out your purpose.

Come along and walk with me as we pray.

## PRAYER WALK
## (STEPS)

**Step 1: (Inhale/Exhale slowly)**

Focus your mind on spiritual things. Thank God for His unconditional love, goodness, mercy, provisions, and ultimate victory. (Just praise Him in the moment.) As the saying goes, "When praises go up, blessings come down."

> Finally, brethren, whatsoever things are true, whatsoever things *are* honest, whatsoever things *are* just, whatsoever things *are* pure, whatsoever things *are* lovely, whatsoever things *are* of good report; if *there be* any virtue, and if *there be* any praise, think on these things.
>
> Philippians 4:8

**Step 2:**

With a contrite spirit, ask God to penetrate your thoughts, enlighten your heart and refresh your spirit. Acknowledge any known sin; sin of commission (knowingly committed), and sin of omission (decline to do right). Ask God to forgive you for all unrighteousness and to become "godly sorrowful" (2 Corinthians 7:10,

NKJV). (Hereto, forgive yourself and continue your prayer request.)

"In all your ways acknowledge Him, and He shall direct your paths" (Proverbs 3:6, NKJV).

"That if thou shalt confess with thy mouth the Lord Jesus, and shalt believe in thine heart that God hath raised him from the dead, thou shalt be saved" (Romans 10:9).

**Step 3:**
Now, ask God to reveal His purpose in your life. Restore the talent, spiritual gifts, creativity, skills, and help minister by stirring up the passion within to enhance the Kingdom of God. Listen attentively; wait for God to speak. Likewise, consecrate and/or identify the divine place to ascertain a blessed life. This positive move will reveal *how* and *where* to serve. (Keep your appointment.)

**Step 4:**
Thank God for His revealing power and the greater work He has begun in you. (Confirmation may come instantly or may be revealed at a later date (as you continue to pray and believe).

"Therefore, if any man be in Christ, he is a new creation; old things have passed away; behold, all things have become new" (2 Corinthians 5:17, NKJV).

"But you are a chosen generation, a royal priesthood, a holy nation, His own special people, that you may proclaim the praises of Him who called you out of darkness into His marvelous light" (1 Peter 2:9, NKJV).

**Lastly:** Tellingly, you have repented (transgressions), reconnected (Christ), resolved (questionable issues) and received (the Good News). Time is at hand for believers and new converts to walk out your divine destiny. By doing so, you will have redirected your path with ordered steps. Now, it is time to pursue and propel.

## POEM:
## "SHEKINAH GLORY"

Flood gates are open, Come and see
Stop and get refreshed; Shekinah Glory
raining down on thee.
The rain is cool and fresh
And will bless your soul
Creating
awareness of wonder
Remarkably to behold.

The healing power soothes the oppressed
To lift your spirit and counteract distress
Of the cares and idiosyncrasies
of the day
Recognize that God is omnipresent
His plans will not decay.
(Jeremiah 29:11)
To rebuild, restore, or remove
any lasting residue of deep despair
(Encrypted with fear, doubt, seclusion)
Make no mistake about it,
God's grace is sufficient anytime and anywhere.

To revive the soul and recapture the spirit of glory
By conviction

Your speech will be bold; your stance will be Holy.
Thereby
Testifying of God's power
in your intellectually awakening hour.
The invigorating water is Holy and Divine
Tellingly, your light will shine.
By deliberate fashion when you get in line
to have your life remarkable refine.

Taking measured steps in walking a straight line
Determined to reach the prescribed goal
with a consecrated mind.

Just as a light that sits on a hill
cannot be hid
Like a beacon of hope to be revealed
Your carnal life will be healed.
When taking hold of the Bread of Life
that is instilled
Instilled in your heart, mind, and soul
The Word of God will make you whole.

Come dine with Jesus as He reigns
while Shekinah Glory falls like rain
Refreshingly, pure, and Holy
will be your tidings to proclaim boldly.
Shekinah Glory raining down, you will see

Expressively revealing showers of excellency
To cleanse your heart
When you earnestly take part;
focus on a new start.
Believing and receiving is a matter of the heart.
Stay alert and do not abort this glorious part
That is,
Jesus Christ, the Redeemer
will give you a fresh start
When embarking on life's journey,
Destined to
Consummate a Divine landmark.

## WHEN IS MY TIME TO PURSUE/PROPEL?

"Propel" is defined as "to drive forward or onward by or as if by means of a force that imparts motion."[17]

You must be contemplating when is it time to realize your dream, vision, and passion that is lying dormant, and yet lurking within your being. An old proverb goes: "Passions are the winds that propel our vessel." For simplicity's sake, you are the vessel and passions are the wind (the driving force behind you).

> "Therefore, if anyone cleanses himself from the latter, he will be a vessel for honor, sanctified, and useful for the Master, prepared for every good work" (2 Timothy 2:21, NKJV).

The time to propel is the appointed time that God has ordained. One must be in tune with the Spirit of God, availing self to respond affirmatively and timely. Do not give space to doubt. Trust God, knowing that His timing is right regardless of your agenda or your desire to postpone the assignment. A timely or untimely response will result in a sweet or bitter outcome—mission accomplished, mission hindered, or perhaps mission abandoned. Self-denial is essential regarding God's timing. However, unless you deny your flesh, please know that the carnal nature impregnates the mind. Pervading thought process—whatever it wants to do (unlimited/timing); and through selfish choice, dictates whichever way you want to do it. This latter act will inevitably cancel or abolish your time to go forth unless you return to a divine place (i.e., a spiritual mindset and a wholesome environment) to be able to properly carry out your mission walk.

The million-dollar question is, "If not now, when?"

Immediately dismiss and do not allow thoughts of doubt, past failures, and disappointments to highjack your progression. The very moment mind/cerebral capacity kindles the realization that the will of man and actions thereof lead to the path of decisions (i.e., good vs. evil; reconciliation vs. conflict; responsible vs. irresponsible actions) triggers a choice to be made. Being convinced, affirmative action and wholesome behavior lead to abundant life, liberty, and the pursuit of happiness. Herein is the genesis of spiritual conception and perseverance.

> "Happy is that people, that is in such a case: yea, happy is that people, whose God is the LORD" (Psalm 144:15).

Since time is of the essence and the timetable of life is limited, without delay, one must rethink the apparent conditions that affect one's wellbeing, such as life, liberty, and the pursuit of happiness. These principles must be pondered and assessed to determine whether you will be traveling down the right road. Take a break! Slow down and decide on life's crossroad signs: a) Abundant life vs. merely existing, b) Perfect law of liberty vs. chains that bind, and c) Joy of the Lord vs. drowning in the sea of wilderness. When you reassess the situation (quality of life) whether it is meaningful or discover it is detrimental; if the latter, redirect your actions, remove distractions, and readjust your mind in charting a more positive pathway geared towards a successful landing. Whatever is hindering and/or dissuading you from reaching divine destiny, remember there may be some things you may have to let go of, and some folks (associates/relationships) to give up in order to move forward in excellence.

> "I press toward the mark for the Prize of the high calling of God in Christ Jesus" (Philippians 3:14).

Purpose and people are primary factors that dictate the time that ordained assignments come to fruition. When man's carnality evokes his own reasoning and challenges (in a false and disguised order) the planned destiny that God preordained, without realignment, brings about unnecessary squalls of tests, tempests of trials, and onslaughts of burdens. With this, doing it "my way" attitude is merely Satan's setup to strategically reel one into a bitter avalanche in life. Satan's strategic plan is to play on the mind (the first battleground of spiritual warfare). Influencing one to think that time stands still when doing your own thing and time is on your side. So, untrue.

People (i.e., relationships/associations, family, friends, cohorts, peers) oftentimes play a key role in sidetracking you in meeting the preordained assignment. Primarily for selfish motives, they would prefer having you to themselves to continue in the same norm; mode of operation (MO). Rather than for you to reassess your perspective in fulfilling your called destiny. On the other hand, oftentimes, the struggles in life are the result of self-inflicting wounds. Careless behaviors exhibited with little or no attempt to correct the unfavorable actions thereof. Unfortunately, contrary action takes precedence over appeals of wise counsel to the detriment of vulnerability at its best.

While on life's journey, human nature has a tendency to look back and revisit bitter experiences that may very well draw you into a cocoon. Thereby, draining daylight into darkness. Be mindful, this will cause you to lose traction and hinder progress in becoming productive. Alternatively, when looking back comes on your radar, reflect on the bitter experiences that bounced the "ounce of faith" to the forefront and markedly propelled you to move forward.

> And Jesus said unto them, Because of your unbelief: for verily I say unto you, if ye have faith as a grain of mustard seed, ye shall say unto this mountain, remove hence to yonder place; and it shall remove; and nothing shall be impossible unto you.
>
> Matthew 17:20

Humanity's life cycle exposes the midnight hour that depicts devastation in one's life. Invaded with sickness, disease(s); immeasurable pain/sorrow; instigated by the adversary to hasten the misfortune. Furthermore, in this driven society, the midnight hour can also rob individuals of a productive life by wreaking untimely death targeted to stop midstream in carrying out one's mission.

Do not be dismayed:

> "Looking unto Jesus the author and finisher of our faith; who for the joy that was set before him endured the cross, despising the shame, and is set down at the right hand of the throne of God" (Hebrews 12:2).

## POEM:
## "WITH GOD, YOU CAN"

The source of sickness is at its peak
Whereas,
The surge of wellness seems quite weak
when dealing with pain, trauma, and seemingly defeat.

Tears flowing on your face like rain,
the objective of Satan's game
to hinder your essence from becoming fame.
Fame not so much to gain
But reclaim the vessel of honor
that has your name.

The pain is deep, penetrating at its peak
Take a sober mind to compete
to stand firm on God's critique,
which is the Word of God that is unique—
Declaring,
A purposeful life without defeat.

Hold on to faith when sickness arises
Knowing that God gave His only Begotten Son to die
To wipe away all tears from your eyes.

His healing virtue will revive
the feeble, broken, and torn soul inside
Without a threat to minimize
His glory, His miracle, and His love
that is sanctioned from above
to give new life symbolic of a dove.

So, get up, look up and live!

When God imparts (speaks to your heart) an ordained assignment, which may be a mission or a position, trust me, you will ultimately know in your intellect, spirit, heart, and soul. Initially, you may not listen attentively and obey. Nevertheless, when you listen with your heart, you will know that HE is the greater I AM. That God is calling you to fulfill a vital destiny appointment.

> "Make you complete in every good work to do His will, working in you what is well pleasing in His sight, through Jesus Christ, *to whom be glory forever and ever. Amen"* **(Hebrews 12:20–21, NKJV).**

It is by choice to listen for and surrender to the clarion call of God. Choose the pathway of abundant life. As you propel, be cognizant of life's walk-through (infiltrated with good and evil). Consistently assess your inner/spiritual infrastructure and soundness of secular environments that directly affect your progress.

**POEM:**
**"LIFE"**

Everybody got a story to tell
Whether it is depicted heavenly
or illustrated as hell.
The story is part of our everyday lives
filled with trials and tribulations
and perhaps even some lies.

Many days made ways to replace the white lies
with readiness to embrace the divine prize,
to honor and accept for the rest of our lives.

Divine prize is pressing toward the calling of God
to be the best that you can be
in His ex-cell-en-cy!

Trials are tests and tests are trials
that provoke you to be strong
wondering where did you go wrong.

Amid the midst of tests and trials
you discover that you are God's child.
Beckoning,

Come my child, take your rest,
you are already blessed.
No need to worry or shed a tear
Jesus Christ, our Savior is already here.
He is as close to you as can be
wrapped in your heart; nearer my God to thee.

Look to the hills from whence cometh your help
God heard you when you first wept.

So, wipe your eyes and be strong
Breakthrough is around the corner
and will not be long.

It is predicated on your faith to:
See the invisible, believe the impossible
and
"Call those things that be not as though they were."

While in your struggle, you must realize
that Jesus is the prize
He will settle all debt
and not leave you compromised.

So, when you look back over your life
counting the times of mix-ups, mess-ups,
fall-downs; get-ups; stalled, quit/gave up;
you will see that Jesus paid the price at

Calvary
so that you can take hold
Immediately
of the Tree of Life
Perpetually!

Free your thoughts and the guilt
to renounce the enemy's relentless steal.
Stealing your integrity, joy, and peace
by the Word of God declare, Satan's release.

If you are sullen due to bad choices made;
resist the devil and make Satan behave.
Lift your chin, hold it up;
head high, look up
Jehovah El Shaddai is more than enough.

Put a smile on your face;
get ready to run the Christian race.
Journeying here and there in a deliberate pace
sanctioned by God's grace.

Remember, my friend,
you still have a chance to expand your story;
make haste and do not waste,
and give God the glory!

To choose the spiritual pathway for a victorious life is secured by trusting God through the good times and bad times. By embracing the plan and purpose of God, sour sentiments and bitter experiences of life transition into a sweet-smelling flower (reality) that is rooted and grounded in the Word of God. With this resolve, your life will be built on a solid rock (Jesus) that will not crack, crumble, capsize, or fail.

Circumspectly, as you move forward discovering your divine place and purpose, providence is decisively enveloped in every stride. Nevertheless, the bittersweet vine of turmoil is: a) claiming your name, b) crawling to the lowest degree to derail your place, and c) climbing to the highest potential to uproot your purpose. By this means, the enemy can ultimately obstruct your divine ending. Regardless of the blazing bitter thrust targeted on life's journey, God's amazing grace blossoms like flowers, but unlike flowers, never dies. It is available and more than able to withstand the storms of life.

CHAPTER 3

# Eye of the Storm

**WATERLOGGED**

When in the eye of the storm, the law of nature asserts: "self-preservation comes first."

"Technically, eye of the storm refers to a false calm at the center of a real or figurative storm (specifically a strong tropical cyclone). However, many writers use it to mean simply middle of the action, where the upheaval is strongest."[18]

In this text, symbolic of a spiritual storm, the phrase "eye of the storm" is used in the same vein, signifying a pivotal point where the situation is bitter, and the upheaval is greatest. When in the eye of the storm (middle of austere situations), the unrelenting pressure of surmountable thunderstorms of unresolved issues, current ordeals, and waves of despair wreak havoc on the individual (vessel). These bitter situations are designed to bombard and intensify a spiritual debacle, subsequently creating a weaken vessel. The minute one's vessel is weak, it clouds the ability to think clearly and to be attuned to the will of God. The greater the storm, the more vehemently it beats against the vessel, which is devised to abolish God's plan and purpose in your life.

Sooner or later, the trail of life most surely will lead to an environment (terrain) that is spiritually stormy, impacting one's stamina. In so doing, it will test your contentment in effectuating your divine place while walking out your purpose, shaping one's destiny. Mind you, as you stroll along through life enjoying God's grace, reminiscing and taking in nature's splendor, happy is he/she. Allow me to remind you not to get too comfortable, given that trouble lurks in darkness. In disguise, the enemy encamps around and about. Suddenly! You are under bitter attack, not because of misdoings, but because the enemy has sought you out. Simply because you are a child of God. Nevertheless, fearlessly through prayer and empowerment of God's Word within, you will be strengthened to remain steadfast by resisting the mental entrapment of doubt, anxiety, and the spirit of giving up, which are stumbling blocks provoked by the adversary.

> "Ye are of God, little children, and have overcome them: because greater is he that is in you, than he that is in the world" (1 John 4:4).

As in the natural landscape of hurricane season, when the eye of the hurricane moves over, the tumultuous effects of the hurricane are felt; then suddenly quietness prevails—giving a false sense of calmness and climatic control. Likened to the natural landscape of the storms of life, there are spiritual landscapes to subdue (i.e., plateaus of problems, plains of pain, hills of havoc, mountains of misery, rivers of restlessness; soil of sadness) that very well may catapult you into the middle of the storm experience.

> "When the enemy shall come in like a flood, the Spirit of the Lord shall lift up a standard against him" (Isaiah 59:19).

## THE "CALM EFFECT"

In Mark 4:35–40, the disciples were on a ship and Jesus had retired in the lower part fast asleep. Prior to boarding the ship to go to the other side of the sea, apparently, the climate was calm. When the tempest commenced rising, the raging wind and waves threatened to overtake their spirit and swallow them at sea. With the ship filled with water, the disciples became fearful, since Jesus was not physically in their midst. They hurriedly awakened him and questioned, "'Master, carest thou not that we perish?' [Jesus] arose and rebuked the wind and said unto the sea, 'Peace, Be Still.' And the wind ceased, and there was a great calm." As a teaching moment, Jesus questioned their fearfulness and lack of faith to redirect the disciples to soul search (genuine belief) and to ascertain their stance in the Word of God.

There was no justifiable reason for the disciples to fear and become fickle. Without a doubt, execution of a grain of faith (as a mustard seed) would have provoked divine omnipotence in their presence to mitigate the situation. That is, if they had not become ensnared in fright. Instead, while in panic, the disciples called for Jesus' (physical presence) to protect them. What the disciples failed to realize is that they were looking at the wind/waves as the destroyer rather than focusing on the Creator. At that very instance, they questioned the Holy Oracles that were taught to them (prior to departing on the voyage) by the greatest teacher/Jesus, the "Word made Flesh." Being unable to maximize the truth of the Word, the disciples succumbed to settling to a much lesser degree.

> "And the Word was made flesh, and dwelt among us, (and we beheld his glory, the glory as of the only begotten of the Father,) full of grace and truth" (John 1:14).

Takeaway: When rocked with storms of entrenching downpours of problematic issues that appear to flood your soul, steadfast faith is essential because the pressures of life enlist itself as a permanent entrapment to war against the spirit. Have faith in God to bring wholeness into your situation. Jesus is the Prince of Peace and is not asleep in the lower part of the ship (your situation). In spirit, Jesus is at the helm waiting for your faith to ignite (through prayer), believing and declaring that it is already done. The storms of life may cause shaking in your body. Nevertheless, by communing with Jesus, you will find rest in your spirit while on board in your heart.

> "Therefore, I say unto you, What things soever ye desire, when ye pray, believe that ye receive them, and ye shall have them" (Mark 11:24).

## POEM:
## "TRAPPED IN THE STORM"

Tempest is raging in the heat of the storm
Mind, body, spirit looking on
Symbolic of a drone with limited power
to mitigate the storm in the hour.

Can't breathe, can't move—paralyzed!
Caught up and hard to look up
when in despair
Unending terror still there.

Appears the enemy is winning...
Unfair!
Miscarriage of faith, hope and charity.
Hard to breathe when in a storm
Breath of fresh air long gone.

Gasping for breath is hard
Like respite, (Holy Spirit) needed to restart
mind, body, and spirit
to break the chain that binds
keeping one spiritually in decline.

Pause and exhale and take some time
Realize that God has equipped you down inside
to deliver from the raging water outside.

Work with the Tools of the Art
Prayer, Power, and Faith-tower
provide deliverance for the hour.

Matter of fact, let us be clear
When the storm is over,
there will be more to undergo.

Opportunity to escape through faith-tower
By prayer request
experience God's power.
Not only during the storm
Also, affectionately amid a perfect calm.

Jesus spoke to the sea when the tempest was high
Declaring, "Peace be still."

As healer of our soul
Regardless of the problem
if you take hold of the banner;
God's Word is the answer.

From hence the day will come
Man will recognize God's plan to overcome
the raging waters that have begun
to overtake life's outcome.

Just as dams hold back raging waters
God's Word shores up his grace and power
To calm your tempest in the hour.

Stop focusing on the storm
Realize God's Son is Liberator for everyone.

**SHAKEN TO REST**

In our carnality (natural life), metaphorically the calm effect can be described (expressed) in two distinguished ways: 1) Inwardly Secret Storm, and 2) Outwardly Bubbling Mask.

## INWARDLY SECRET STORM

Internally suppressed is a silent storm. Many people suffer in secret without disclosing their pain or displaying the grip of spiritual disparity and the uncomfortable heaviness felt within while in the heat of the storm. Difficult times and exacerbated experiences may very well elicit a bitter battle of depression, causing isolation, spirit shaken, and ultimately setting up for self-pity-party. The mind is bewildered, hoping no one will discern the stress that is left as a residue of the unrelenting mess. Emotions in overdrive, desperately trying to appear all right; desperately yearning to go outside to be alone; anywhere so no one will hear the groan.

There is no rest for the weary and no words to utter except questioning God, in the midst, with little or, if any, concentration of what is murmured. All the same, the mind is perplexed, eyes are dimmed, and the spirit is exasperated, slowly slumbering into a dark place while teetering on the edge of night. Physical movement is at a minimum, embracing the window of opportunity to slumber and sleep. To act as if this despondent behavior is therapy, which is misconstrued and utilized to escape from constructively responding to the issues of life. Eventually the curtains are closed, lights go out, and there you are—bewildered, overcome with roller-coaster emotions. The trumpet of seclusion sounds. By shrewd means, your voice is concealed, as a silencer, to perturb the soul. Mere intellect appears to be frozen in time; soundness escapes into an abyss, with no recollection of sanity to discern the hour.

If truth be told, there are believers suffering in silence; hereinafter referred to as Suffering Saints (SS). Without question, they feel there is no one to confide in or anyone who understands. There are some spiritual storms that will silence one to sleep when in the depth of despair (1 Corinthians 13:12, 1 Peter 4:12). For the most part, these SS struggle with the tempest of tests/trials that threaten their very voice to silence. Thereto, overthrown positive actions drown in the sea of hush-hush despair, succumbing to reticent behavior and gut-wrenching loneliness.

## POEM: "LONELINESS"

Loneliness is like walking through an underground cave,
where darkness to cold is as bleak and dim
as the infrastructure.
Where crevices of surrounding rocks permeate
a cold draft into one's presence.
It is where streams of water trickle down the stony walls—
nothing more than the tears streaming down your face.
Each teardrop represents a weak heartbreak
that ultimately unfolds into dry eyes in the dark.

"Those that sow in tears shall reap in joy" (Psalm 126:5).

Even though engulfed in despair, the Word of God that is planted in your heart awakens, reminding you are not alone. The Scripture says: "The word is near you, in your mouth and in your heart" (Romans 10:8, NKJV).

As you hold on, rays of hope illuminate while the bitter bud of darkness dissipates. Tears of joy stream down your face, seemingly as mighty as the great Niagara Falls. Empowered to reclaim your voice and spiritual stamina; the scripture speaks in our stead. "Likewise the Spirit also helps in our weaknesses. For we do not know what we should pray for as we ought, but the Spirit Himself makes intercession for us with groanings which cannot be uttered" (Romans 8:26, NKJV).

## OUTWARD APPEARANCE

The walk, the talk—the overall disposition displays normality. The prevailing spirit working overtime, desperately masking the hidden man/woman (the very person) experiencing the inward/silent storm. Herein, the outward persona appears to be calm; but, yet, inwardly there is a raging tempest. Oftentimes, SS gives a stellar natural performance in their associations and interactions with others, but what is spiritually transparent is the façade of the performance. This action seeks to garner a stamp of approval from man without exposure regarding the cause. However, do not be dismayed. Do you not know the perils of life are permitted to strengthen one for the journey?

Every individual has a race to run, a different road to travel, and various obstacles to encounter. Cognitive seclusion of spiritual virtues exacerbates becoming improperly dressed. Slumbering in an identity crisis and barely functioning with ill-fitting spiritual tools will lead to premature disaster. Immersing in spiritual warfare infiltrating the senses appear to be winning, but God! This, my friend, is when it is time to rebuke the adversary in the Name of Jesus and declare victory into your situation. Victory is ultimately yours when a sound mindset is prevalent. This concentration will fortify steadfastness and faith in God while making positive adjustments to counteract the wrong.

> Then they cried to the Lord in their trouble, and he delivered them from their distress. He made the storm be still, and the waves of the sea were hushed. Then they were glad that the waters were quiet, and he brought them to their desired haven.
>
> Psalm 107:28–30 (ESV)

## OUTWARDLY/BUBBLING MASK (ASSOCIATION VS. ASSIMILATION)

Without a steadfast commitment to eliminate the sea of diminishing returns, for a season, many people will seek to escape hard times by aligning themselves with religious and social organizations. By taking on their culture; unfortunately, they lose their personal identity. "When it comes to living in a hostile culture, many Christians choose either assimilation or separation.

Assimilation means you gradually look like everyone else. Their values become your values; your lifestyle imitates theirs."[19]

Keeping the "I" going in various walks of life, individuals continue to connect with various organizations, institutions, and committees. Furthermore, they participate in family and social gatherings, attempting to avoid the stigma of the spiritual storm plaguing their inner soul rather than embrace transparency and truth. Above all, settling in a wholesome place and being true to oneself allows the opportunity to become confidently transparent. This is accomplished by sorting out challenged and unresolved issues that have become a burial ground within your heart. Headstones of loneliness, hopelessness, pain, weakness, unforgiveness, and insecurities plague humanity. These are feelings temporarily concealed by a masquerade of normalcy. However, a sure way to overcome these distresses is to ask God to regulate the circumstances long enough to rediscover inner serenity (rest for your soul), which rewards spiritual clarity.

> For which cause, we faint not; but though our outward man perish yet the inward man is renewed day by day. For our light affliction, which is but for a moment, worketh for us a far more exceeding and eternal weight of glory.
>
> 2 Corinthians 4:16–17

In the average lifespan, there will be imminent wilderness days to experience. Unfortunately, an ambiance of normality takes hold only to last for a season. The climate periodically revives, presenting a refreshing and rejoicing time; it positionally appears that the storm is passing over. (The calm before the storm.) Before you know it, raging winds of discomfort and the overwhelming relentless rains of life find their way back to your door. To that end, the bittersweet fog looms in to mark reality. Sweeping winds of despair cradled with valley lows assault personal affairs that are critical to your spiritual survival. Failure to take your hands off and put these matters in the Master's Hand will result in dis-ease consequences. Be that as it may, and do understand by lying dormant, a dark cloud of life's boulders reappears, while a busting breeze of provocation erupts to intimidate one's mind and distort positive actions—satanically sanctioned on this emotionally rainy day, beating intensely upon your will. What is more, sanity and endurance are under attack to cease and lose heart.

> "And let us not be weary in well doing: for in due season we shall reap, if we faint not" (Galatians 6:9).

By denial, within the fabrication of a happy home mindset and an absence of deep spiritual cleansing and increasing faith to endure, one remains chained with weights/burdens, and entrapment in the eye of the storm. Without a real commitment (mindset) and gospel plan in place to conform to, postures an anti-spiritual house built in the sand, void of a solid foundation.

> And everyone that heareth these sayings of mine, and doeth them not, shall be likened unto a foolish man, which built his house upon the sand: And the rain descended, and the floods came, and the winds blew, and beat upon that house; and it fell: and great was the fall of it.
>
> Matthew 7:26–27

Crafted within the God-given celestial cavity constituting inner strength and perseverance, the will to live is greater than the threat to die. Will outweighs struggle and struggle outweighs pain. The degree of the intensity of pain is predicated on how one sees and deals with struggle. Reclaim the reservoir of hope and inner strength within by asking God for help, and His Will (purpose) will be realized in your life.

> "When you go through deep waters, I will be with you. When you go through rivers of difficulty, you will not drown. When you walk through the fire of oppression, you will not be burned up; the flames will not consume you" (Isaiah 43:2, NLT).

Spiritual intuitiveness resolutely stimulates a disposition that reflects a renewed mindset to be still and trust God to abandon the mask. This will be accomplished by walking in the newness of life, full of grace, truth, and tranquility.

## POEM:
## "GOD'S GRACE"

Growing green grass is like God's grace.
As long as grass is watered and the sun shines on it, the grass gets greener and greener and lives longer.

Likewise, as long as the Son (of God) shines on your life,
you grow in grace, life becomes fuller, and you live spiritually refreshingly longer.

My sisters/brothers, as you stand on what you know concerning God's grace, promises, and provisions, only in His timing, figuratively, spiritual mountains are made low.

> "Thou hast caused men to ride over our heads; we went through fire and through water; but thou broughtest us out into a wealthy place" (Psalm 66:12).

With a sound mind, while simultaneously maintaining a wholesome place, nothing would be able to overtake you. God's grace serves as an anchor when billows roar, flawlessly survival-ready.

Come unto me, all ye that labour and are heavy laden, and I will give you rest. Take my yoke upon you, and learn of me; for I am meek and lowly in heart: and ye shall find rest unto your souls. For my yoke is easy, and my burden is light.

Matthew 11:28–30

CHAPTER 4

# Weather the Storm

**STEADFAST POWER**

"That He would grant you, according to the riches of His glory, to be strengthened with power through His Spirit in the inner self" (Ephesians 3:16, NASB).

Weather-the-storm (verb/idiomatic). "To reach the end of a very difficult situation without too much harm or damage."[20]

Weather-the-storm defined: "To be able to continue doing something despite serious problems."[21]

The latter definition is in keeping with the subject. What do you do while in the storm? Certainly not murmuring and complaining! Murmuring and complaining arouse more misery and contaminate the environment with an acidic energy that stalemates spiritual awakening. For seasoned believers, this type of behavior should be a thing of the past. Resting in God is like basking in His favor. You have learned how to stand still and see the liberation of the Lord. A pious and steadfast attitude is likened to a spiritual general in the Army of the Lord that refuses to take down. As an old gospel spiritual declares, "Victory, victory, shall be mine. If I hold out and let the Lord fight my battle, I know victory shall be mine."

Withstanding the storm calls for putting on traveling shoes of endurance. With the issues of life, the lesson learned is to trust God and wait for His timing. More often than not, the wait may be long, uncomfortable, painful, and perhaps you may even experience some setbacks. Nevertheless, while on the wait list, a fleeting attitude of uncertainty can very well come into play, simply causing your patience to become drained, lurking on the edge of emptiness amid bumps of doubt assaulting your spiritual stance.

Keeping it real, there is never the desire to wait for anything or wait on anybody based on the proposed allotment of time concerning one's personal interest. If anything threatens one's personal timetable, it will influence a wavering mindset that will ultimately facilitate a ghastly experience. However, in the school of God's Word, the mighty intellect is no longer carnally driven, but divinely enlightened. That said, the wait then becomes intentional, entrenched with the prevailing attitude of expectation/anticipation.

The motivational spiritual elements propel one to a heart of thanksgiving and praise concerning what God has already done. You will cease not to pray and will continue looking forward to the promises of God. As the elevation of praise exudes the atmosphere, the evidence of the Word of God penetrates the heart and banishes the seed of doubt that was sown to diminish the essence of hope.

The process of evaluation (self-assessment) and determination (willpower) are serious qualities to retain. Thus, equipping you to propel to the next spiritual level. This level represents having unyielding faith in God. Faith tramps doubt, knowing that God is everything you need in every situation. That is, as you fasten your eyes on God and connect to His heart as He holds your hand. With that, tests and trials are defeated when you walk in faith, stillness, and joy. By doing so, those former bittersweet experiences enhance a deeper desire to trust God even more while moving forward.

> "But they that wait upon the Lord shall renew their strength; they shall mount up with wings as eagles; they shall run, and not be weary; and they shall walk and not faint" (Isaiah 40:31).

Whether in natural or spiritual parameter, preparedness ranks number one in combatting the forces of storms that result in discomfort and vile consequences. Preparation may be evaluated by three factors to consider: 1) Obtainability, 2) Responsibility, and 3) Endurability, which are vital qualities in withstanding the storm.

## OBTAINABILITY

"Obtainability," according to dictionary.com; "to come into possession of; get, acquire, or procure, as through an effort or by a request."[22] While enduring a natural storm, essential supplies (i.e., goods, first aid kit, tools, etc.) are warranted. Every household should have a game plan and a suitable supply inventory for unexpected stormy situations. As soon as the forecast of severe weather is broadcast, procure and store adequate supplies before crowds of consumers arrive at the supermarket and deplete the supplies on the shelves. Because of that, this proactive effort will mitigate many anticipated problems. However, in the spiritual realm, just in case you are worn-out with waves of worry, darkness of despair, and countless calamities, now is the time to avail yourself in quietness and meditation to hear the voice of God. Prayer and praise, worship, and the Word are spiritual weapons to stockpile in getting through the storm.

Waving the red flag! In stormy weather, fasten your eyes on God.

> "I will lift up mine eyes to the hills, from when cometh my help. My help cometh from the Lord, which made heaven and earth" (Psalm 121:1–2).

> "Let us therefore come boldly unto the throne of grace, that we may obtain mercy, and find grace to help in time of need" (Hebrews 4:16).

During these arduous times, cry out to God until the Holy Spirit ignites your mind, heart, and soul. As your inner man is saturated, you do not have to wait. Take your victory lap now, being assured that the storm is passing over and heavenly stars are aligning in favor. Subsequently, the dismal dark cloud, integrated with cosmological atmosphere pressure, will be recanted under the Mighty Hand of God that forced it to cease its path of dilemma and destruction. Prayer forced the storm to bow. Praise forced it to slumber. Worship forced the storm to retreat, and the Word slew the stronghold.

## RESPONSIBILITY

Responsibility—As referenced, "the ability or authority to act or decide on one's own, without supervision." [23] Designated people who have been assigned to carry out specific tasks during the storm are expected to take responsibility and carry out their tasks. Everyone should work in alliance with one another and in a timely manner to be successful in reaching the delegated goal. Periodic rehearsals are commendable in being proactive to ensure everyone is proficient and prepared instead of waiting until the storm arrives.

From a spiritual perspective, prior to the storm of life rages, pray consistently and be thankful for God's grace/mercy to take one day at a time. Likewise, maintain responsibility for one's actions through transparency by taking ownership of past failures, yet knowing you are an overcomer through Christ Jesus. Prayer, meditation, and acknowledgement of indiscretions are vital to clear the way for an open line of communication and communion with God. By being committed to this prescribed course of action, it will keep you spiritually sustainable in times of trouble. Say goodbye to the nine pounds of steel (whatever it is) that is keeping you chained and bound, and learn to travel light. Jesus said,

"For My yoke is easy and My burden is light" (Matthew 11:30, NKJV).

> "Let us lay aside every weight, and the sin which doth so easily beset us, and let us run with patience the race that is set before us" (Hebrews 12:1).

## ENDURABILITY

Endurability: "The state of being endurable."[24] Endurance: "The ability to withstand hardship or adversity especially: the ability to sustain a prolonged stressful effort or activity; The act or an instance of enduring or suffering endurance of many hardships."[25] Endurance is symbolic of a life jacket in weathering the storm. From the natural perspective, medical conditions, physical strength, and the state of one's mind are prerequisites in determining roles and responsibilities a person would hold when facing the storm. Feebleness and incoherent individuals, to say the least, cancel them out for physical activity assignments, etc. Given the situation, overall physical ability and medical soundness are vital to ensure that if a storm becomes so severe as to require bodily strength and mental endurance capability is there to maintain survival in the storm.

Likewise, spiritual discernment recognizes intercessors that need not be primed or pumped in times like these. Everyone exhibits varied attributes/sensitivities commensurate with their spiritual maturity and/or physical abilities. However, regardless of who you are, etc., it is expedient for everyone to have praise in their mouth and prayer in their heart. Check your personal pantry for prayer and portal for praise; wardrobe for worship; and wet appetite for the Word. Do not be at ease until you have a full supply. By utilizing these continually, you will garner endurance. Armed with these spiritual weapons will be the sustainer until strengthened indeed. Mighty Child of God, now you are outfitted to stand still and see the liberation of the Lord.

> "In times of trouble, may the Lord answer your cry. May the name of God of Jacob keep you safe from all harm" (Psalm 20:1, NLT).

In such severe and frightening situations, once the storm has ceased, it is essential to go out and assess whether the storm wreaked any physical damage on personal property or neighbors' property and the community as a whole. Predicated on the severity of the storm, when deemed safe, provide aid to neighbors in lending a helping hand to repair, rebuild, etc., which will be a collaborative effort. This type of camaraderie is typical in our society today—neighbors helping neighbors in times of trouble. Above all, strive to continue that genuine concern and support when the storm has ceased. Be not amazed by working together in natural endeavors; communication, collaboration and unity are precious during tests of times. Consequently, in many instances, unneighborly behavior subsides and long-lasting friendships develop because of these bittersweet experiences.

"In everything give thanks: for this is the will of God in Christ Jesus concerning you" (1 Thessalonians 5:18).

For the most part, your spiritual armor is God (the ultimate source) that will truly stand. Besides, when surviving spiritual storms, one must first look inside one's self. This is the opportunity to tap into the reservoir of greatness that is within. Retrieve the treasure chest of gospel teachings, spiritual songs, and hymns to renew your spirit and lift you up, exemplifying faith that God will deliver. Child of God, you are an overcomer, and as you walk circumspectly before God, He will exalt you above the enemy to serve as your footrest. As man is shaped in the image of God, in His infinite wisdom, inherently a touch of greatness is deposited in every individual. To kindle greatness, you must desire to be better in every aspect of life and strive to perform in excellence.

The biggest culprit is assault on oneself inwardly echoing, man isn't perfect; only to use as escapism to settle for mediocrity rather than a more excellent way. When you commence and subsequently stop operating in excellence, the mission crumbles and deteriorates; thus, losing spiritual fragrance. Once divine fragrance is compromised, it leaves you vulnerable and open for stormy attacks from the enemy. The Christian walk must be an example for the building up of God's kingdom. To accomplish this spiritual paradigm, believers must be mindful of our speech (idle words); environments and interactions to be influential (as witnesses) to those who have not yet committed to this spiritual benchmark. That is, a life dedicated to ensuring divine place, fulfilling divine purpose, while simultaneously effectuating divine destiny. In turbulent times, our first inclination is to ask for God's help. To receive the fullness of God across the board, trust His glorious presence and power to withstand the storms of life.

As we strive for perfection, the ointment of excellence is like morning dew that softly rains down from the heavenlies and rests comfortably on its destination without the threat to abort its mission. One must become consciously aware of his/her spiritual place (mindset), and physical place (environment) to maintain honorable consistency regarding your actions while waiting for God to deliver during these perilous times.

In harmony with being spiritually focused, excellence embodies a celestial covering that permeates spiritual and physical places. It is interwoven in the make-up of humanity that flows from God. Since mankind is created by HIM and in HIM, the creative nature of humanity is rooted in greatness. Allow the excellence of God to saturate your mind and environment to ensure that your house is built on the Rock of Jesus and your setting is covered under the Blood. When He sees the blood on your spiritual doorpost, the enemy of despair/trouble will pass over in a subordinate degree. There are times when a complete breakthrough seems impossible; nevertheless, trouble diminishes. Faith is essential during these pressurized times. As you continue to grow spiritually in patience and perseverance (as you wait), God's hand will be revealed in the storm. Once again, the Holy Spirit highjacked the deadly/bitter plan of the adversary. Remember, God is perpetually in control, and we must put our entire trust in Him.

Apart from God, it is not humanly possible to create a human being. Life is in the blood and the excellence of God is integrated in the life-giving blood. When God blew breath into man, He also blew greatness; the embodiment of excellence. That is why every man, woman, boy, and girl should strive to walk (by choice) in excellence that will propel a divine execution. Furthermore, sometimes, evidence of greatness (i.e., gifts, talents, creativity, etc.) must wait to be refined before it is revealed.

> Thou shalt increase my greatness, and comfort me on every side.
>
> Psalm 71:21

> His divine power has granted to us all things that pertain to life and godliness, through the knowledge of him who called us to his own glory and excellence, by which he has granted to us his precious and very great promises, so that through them you may become partakers of the divine nature, having escaped from the corruption that is in the world because of sinful desire.
>
> 2 Peter 1:3–4 (ESV)

## POEM:
## "TOUCH OF GREATNESS"

"Greatness is compared to water as water compared to a well."

Well water is good for your health
Whereas greatness is good for your soul.

Well water tastes better than city water
It is natural.

Oh, taste and see that the Lord is good
He is spiritual.

Just like you dig a well to extract water
You must seek God to discover and empower greatness.

As water is at the bottom of the well
Greatest is at the innermost part of your soul.
It is like drawing water from a well
To retrieve water, one must dip down for it

To receive greatness, one must stand up for it
not bowing to a lesser degree.

At the bottom, water is pure, clean, cool
no contamination because it comes out of the ground
the cradle of the earth.
At the top, greatness is flawless, invigorating
dressed in anointing because Jesus is a well of living water
and life's bucket hangs, not on a rope, but on a sure foundation.

Therefore, thus saith the LORD God, Behold, I lay in Zion for a foundation a stone, a tried stone, a precious corner stone, a sure foundation: he that believeth shall not make haste.

Isaiah 28:16

He that believeth on me, as the scripture hath said, out of his belly shall flow rivers of living water.

John 7:38

As the storm passes over, daybreak arises with such great illumination that darkness has to flee. Keep your traveling shoes on and journey with me a little farther. Do not fall by the wayside. Too close to stop now. Hold your head up, shoulders back, neck and back straight, and feet firm, grounded on the solid rock. Have a drink of living water and inhale the sweet-smelling Savior.

"For in him we live, and move, and have our being; as certain also of your own poets have said, For, we are also his offspring" (Acts 17:28).

I know. The way has been cumbersome. To some degree, bearable; and oftentimes seemingly agonizing. In times like these, it is certainly a weary journey. From time to time, trekking down one road or another, veering into dark roads of despair, lanes of loneliness, streets of sadness likened to tunnels of trouble/bridges of burdens. Yet, through it all, in discovering your divine place, God has always been by your side, serving as a bridge over troubled water.

"Therefore, my beloved brethren, be ye steadfast, unmovable, always abounding in the work of the Lord, forasmuch as ye know that your labor is not in vain in the Lord" (1 Corinthians 15:58).

## POEM:
## "RAINWATER"

Awake my dear from despair
As you regroup for a breath of fresh air.

Spirit is filled with toils of the day
Ready for intensity of night to go away.

Flowing tears like rain
igniting the soul to mitigate the pain.
The ordeal of the day seems to come to stay
Reaping havoc on mind, body, and soul
Waiting for the Holy Spirit to take control.
As rainwater taps against the window seal
The evil spirit lurks and is out for the kill.
Clouds upload with rainwater
While our eyes flood with tears
hoping the tears (disguised as rain water)
will camouflage and drown the fears
long enough to absorb and behold
the well of living water to be revealed.
.
As the clouds release the rain
Tears refrain and embrace the
Clouds of Joy in Jesus Name.

Give up to doubt and search your soul
and allow the Holy Spirit to take control.

To unveil
the love, perseverance, and peace within.

To comprehend
that God never lost a battle and you will win.

"With God,
we are more than conquerors."

We are too close to the finish line. Take this last sprint with me. Almost there! So far on this amazing journey, we have explored My Place and Your Place. Together hand in hand, it is time to explore mankind's quest, as a whole, Our Place; realizing that no man is an island. It still takes a Society. Simply put, a World!

CHAPTER 5

# Our World— Discovering Our Place

**NATIONAL PROCLAMATION**

"WE THE PEOPLE," in this stressful country, are different (i.e., race, gender, creed, religion, etc.), but more importantly, we are inherently the same. Being created in God's image and His likeness regardless of life's cultures, experiences, and transitions (bitter or sweet), the spiritual part of man longs for the intimacy with his Creator. From the inception of creation, every individual is born with a purpose to fulfill. Wherever the geographical area (i.e., local, national, universal) one resides or frequents, it is incumbent for every individual to seek the plan that God has set before him/her. All-encompassing, thriving, and enjoying the abundant life and blessed hope in Christ Jesus. Not only is the divine plan of God for humanity to worship and serve Him, but by posterity create a wholesome village of family and community. In so doing, live in harmony with one another for generations to come. By embracing this divine order, God will bestow supernatural resources and provisions to be successful in establishing and maintaining such a treasured society.

> "The counsel of the LORD stands forever, the plans of his heart to all generations" (Psalm 33:11, ESV).

## PREAMBLE TO THE CONSTITUTION OF THE UNITED STATES

As ratified in "The Constitution of the United States of America."[26]

"WE THE PEOPLE," of the United States, in Order to form a more perfect Union, establish Justice, insure domestic Tranquility, provide for the common defense, promote the general Welfare, and secure the Blessings of Liberty to our-selves and our Posterity, do ordain and establish this Constitution for the United States of America."

In perusal of the Constitution of the United States of America, it is apparent that when the authors penned this great proclamation it signified assurance in the preeminent Word of God. That the Country (America) would be founded on moral and equitable principles to ensure justice, freedom, and to promote and maintain peace and the general welfare for all. Notwithstanding, the authors' intentions are somewhat envisioned; they rightly certified that we the people will enjoy a wholesome life without systematic disparity (in the natural realm) as a whole. As we know, our physical state of affairs has a significant bearing (positive vs. negative) upon our innermost being and livelihood. Sooner or later, the diabolical system of inequity must be settled. The overall principle denotes provision, protection, equality, and inclusion for all people; whereas established and entwined in the fabric of the Constitution.

Unfortunately, encumbered with racial, healthcare, and social injustices; deprivation; crumbling political and moral structure; along with disproportionate economic growth, inevitably escalates to immeasurable ruin. The greatest impact regarding the diminishing level of positive return (in this recycle system), produces homelessness, family separation, impoverished people and communities, unskilled workers, substandard education, and polarization, to name a few. Enormous discriminatory practices plague the weaker vessels of our society. The underprivileged and disenfranchised are members of the human-body (humanity) just as those placed in higher socioeconomic classifications. More too often, the face of reality begs to differ.

> "For there is no respect of persons with God" (Romans 2:11).

There are so many earth-shattering things that are happening in our country today, from climate change—uncontrollable winter storms (i.e., floods, utility outages), wildfires, horrific hurricanes, tornadoes, devastating landslides/earthquakes—to mass shootings, all in the face of peaceful protests vs. outrageous riots that eventually propelled into "Insurrection of the U.S. Capitol." All occurring concurrently while traveling the uncharted waters of a deadly (100-year) pandemic not long ago experienced. As a result, innumerable COVID–19 cases remain, and well over half a million lives have been lost (at the time of this writing) that left families/friends distraught. With the immeasurable suffering and vast economic decline, no genuine resolve was imminent (prior to, at the time, a new administration) to mitigate and/or abate extensive suffering and death. The nation's chief investment must be in humanity. In that, the return investment of humankind will eventually yield a more wholesome living (i.e., social/economic justice, human rights) and a thriving economy.

> Thus, speaketh the LORD of hosts, saying, execute true judgment, and shew mercy and compassion every man to his brother: And oppress not the widow, nor the fatherless, the stranger, nor the poor; and let none of you imagine evil against his brother in your heart.
>
> Zechariah 7:9–10

While the first excerpt of the Constitution, "…in Order to form a more perfect Union," is reflective, the integrity of this expression, and the actions thereof, appear to have slipped into dismal reality.

## SPIRITUAL DIRECTIVE

Certainly, no individual can reach this goal within oneself. It takes the supreme power of the Most High to tear down walls of intellectual autonomy that exalt itself against the oracles of God. As a believer, when one accepts Christ as their personal savior, the scripture teaches that we are, "Buried with him in baptism, wherein also ye are risen with him through the faith of the operation of God, who hath raised him from the dead" (Colossians 2:12).

The carnal mind is regenerated and transformed in Christ.

> The phrase "in Christ" thus, has a corporate meaning as well: "those in the community of Christ." Communion with Christ necessarily involves a social dimension, experiencing the shared life of his body. This community is defined by its relation to its representative head. Being "in Christ" is thus new life shared in community with those who are related to Christ.[27]

The greatest testament of love by our heavenly Father, through his Son, Jesus, made it possible to have this perfect union with one another. In so doing, it establishes a more perfect union (on all levels) of family, neighborhoods, and communities (i.e., government, church, and state), encompassing country. So that all people will have the opportunity to realize true liberty and the pursuit of happiness without any form of hindrance and systematic bias.

Agape love is defined as: Agape (Ancient Greek pronounced uh-GAH-pay) is a Greco-Christian term referring to love, "the highest form of love, charity" and "the love of God for [human beings] and of [human beings] for God." Within Christianity, agape is considered to be the love originating from God or Christ for humankind.[28]

All the same, agape love and divine union represent the hallmark of the Trinity (God the Father, God the Son, and God the Holy Spirit). This truth speaks to the nature of God that was embodied in Jesus, the Christ, when the Word was made flesh.

> "And the Word was made flesh, and dwelt among us, (And we beheld his glory, the glory as the only begotten of the Father), full of grace and truth" (John 1:14).

Prior to His journey's end on earth, Jesus prayed to the Father for oneness. Oneness for "we the people" to be one (in unity) with each other, and oneness with

God. In that vein, oneness will be expressed and exemplified not only in a vertical relationship (with God via Jesus), but horizontally, as well; forming and consummating a genuine relationship with our fellowman.

> "That they all may be one, as You, Father, are in Me, and I in You; that they also may be one in Us, that the world may believe that you sent Me" (John 17:21, NKJV).

However, in due course, when the enemy of divisiveness is defeated and victory is won by the Mighty Hand of God, the State of the Union will truly be whole.

## POEM:
## "TOGETHER WE STAND"

The sky is blistering with violent cries.
Morning sadness and dreadful nights.

Atmosphere polluted with grave unrest—
Never mind the arsenal of disrespect.

Matters not who you are
Black, white, brown, or red
Assorted ill behavior is a dread.
You say you are Christian
Who said that?
Believers of the gospel our standing act.

Then rise-up believers and claim your spot
that is tattooed on God's hand is the heavenly mark.
Denounce the evil and the wrong
Truth regardless of who is wrong.

Truth is neither black nor white
with no grey area in sight.
So, let us join together and stop the fight
Declaring decency that what is right!

Be opened to compromise and find common ground
And let us stay united as we abound.
Speaking truth to power is our aim
Honoring the Constitution as we proclaim.

## EXCERPTS OF THE PREAMBLE (NARRATIVE):

## ESTABLISH JUSTICE:

It is crucial that the governing parties of these United States come together and collectively agree to uphold every aspect of the Constitution in order to form a more perfect union. Hence, carnal minds must be changed on a divine/spiritual level to attain the expected end as decreed in the Constitution of the United States of America. This pressurize process is by no means easy to accomplish. More often than not, it is a bitter road to travel.

Rightfully, government and political officials must ensure a wholesome environment (i.e., socioeconomic issues, healthcare, social justice, etc.) to safeguard the integrity of our Constitution. Even in partisan situations, statesmen should be able to disagree without becoming disagreeable for the good of the state and country. We the people must turn from a contentious persona gripped in dark chambers of conduct that allows dysfunctional behavior. Aside from that, evoke a spirit of readiness to spring into sunshine of trust and transparency, indicative of a collaborative effort. Besides, staying focused on truth (God's Word) rather than partisan ties will lead to a more productive and wholesome society.

As history repeats itself in a malignant manner, half-heartedly resolving the issues at hand; sorry to say, the bittersweet vine of injustice has marched, spread, and uprooted the very principles of our Constitution and seared the consciousness of man. A call for divine justice is needed. Only then will mankind fully commit and advance to a divine place of established justice for all the people.

> "But let justice roll down like waters, and righteousness like an ever-flowing stream" (Amos 5:24, ESV).

## ENSURE DOMESTIC TRANQUILITY:

Rather than conforming to orderly/regulatory mandates of local/state governments, the audacity of public defiance and tumultuous incidents (protests) continue to destroy not only our cities' infrastructure, but, in many instances, innocent lives. These despicable actions appear to be frozen in the consciousness of man. Yet, the innocent continue to march peacefully, pray secretly, and praise openly. Regardless of how well things are going or how difficult despite, "we the people" are rediscovering no man is an island. Truth is, we are our brother's keeper! As a nation, "we the people," must reconnect and discover our divine place to support one another and walk in the newness of life. By doing so, denounce the evil and inequality that plague our society and vote accordingly. As Christians, we must walk in divine purpose, as ordained by God and prescribed in the Holy Scriptures, henceforth, as we pledge our faith.

> "Fulfil ye my joy, that ye be likeminded, having the same love, being of one accord, of one mind. Let nothing be done through strife or vainglory; but in lowliness of mind let each esteem other better than themselves" (Philippians 2:2–3).

## PROVIDE FOR THE COMMON DEFENSE:

From a nationwide standpoint and globally as well, "we the people" have experienced and/or heard of rumors of wars. In a man's world, in order to exercise the privilege of freedom, preservation had to be made to enjoy it. The carnal struggle always comprises mental, emotional, and physical combats. There were battles to fight, enemies to conquer, and victories to be won. Some warriors were captured; others bled and died apart from those who returned home. Some healthy, others mentally challenged and physically disabled. Many wounded, and yet alive. Countless men and women sacrificed their lives to secure and sustain America's freedom, inclusive of other countries. The same holds true today.

> And ye shall hear of wars and rumours of wars; see that ye be not troubled: for all these things must come to pass, but the end is not yet. For nation shall rise against nation and kingdom against kingdom: and there shall be famines, and pestilences, and earthquakes, in diverse places.
>
> Matthew 24:6–7

Unfortunately, as the world turns, more often than not, it takes a devastating toll on the best of our people. And for the most part, from a spiritual perspective (i.e.,

Christian Soldier) it involves warfare between spirit and carnality (flesh/body) that assault one's beliefs and values. At any rate, succumbing to temptation kindles interactions that compromise the integrity of one's soul.

> "And I will give them a heart to know me, that I am the Lord: and they shall be my people, and I will be their God: for they shall return unto me with their whole heart" (Jeremiah 24:7).

Under pressure, the fight to overcome and not submit to subordinate thought processes in which one was trained is indicative of a loyal soldier. The malicious acts of the enemy come to arrest the human body, brainwash the mind, and infiltrate the spirit. (Threat: to become dishearteningly fearful). Nevertheless, the enemy does not have the power to capture the human soul. The soul of man belongs to God and one day will return to the God that gave it. Even in seasons when the enemy returns, "we the people" are equipped with resilience and resolve, knowing we are more than conquerors through Christ Jesus. In the wilderness of warfare, (natural or spiritual), ask the greatest heavenly warrior, Jesus, for the battle plan, directing execution with precision.

"So do not fear, for I am with you: do not be dismayed, for I am your God. I will strengthen you and help you; I will uphold you with my righteous right hand" (Isaiah 41:10, NIV).

## PROMOTE THE GENERAL WELFARE:

During these perplexing times, it is the perfect opportunity for each of us to consider our personal state of affairs. This can be accomplished by making positive adaptations whenever needed to ensure overall wellbeing of our spiritual and physical health comprising mind, body, and soul. As truthful contemplation commences and purposeful adjustments are made, in and with our lives, realizing that only until the rebellious man (humanity) returns to God, the natural man will continually experience an emptiness of spiritual strength, solace, and peace.

> "Blessed is the nation whose God is the Lord; and the people whom he hath chosen for his own inheritance" (Psalm 33:12).

The lenses of reality mirror a world system that refuses to reach out (with unbiassed and selfless hands) and touch humanity (as a whole) to make this world a better place. Nevertheless, the troubles of this world do not eradicate the power of a sovereign God.

> "He ruleth by his power for ever; his eyes behold the nations: let not the rebellious exalt themselves. Selah" (Psalm 66:7).

Every day is an opportunity to get houses in order—my house, your house, our house, and let us not forget the State House. This is a critical and opportune time in life (history) to change the game plan. Make crooked roads (entangled ideas, biased laws, and practices, etc.) straight by transforming one's mind and actions (individually and collectively), while holding fast to the principles of the Word of God, which is the framework of the Constitution. To get a closer look is to capture what is really going on in society so as to make the necessary adjustments to be better and do better in the home, community, and as a nation.

A progressive (sacred) lens is vital to attain spiritual enlightenment to restore and secure mankind's God-given right of life, liberty, and the pursuit of happiness, regardless of race, creed, or color. God has provided a way to escape a life of hopelessness and despair by obeying and trusting in Him to experience a transformed life. Only when "we the people" become serious about our faith relative to Christian values, as the Holy Bible proclaims, the fabric of our conscious actions (on every level) will be reflective first, by respecting each other, and truthfully revealed by honoring every aspect of the Constitution.

"Teacher, which is the great commandment in the law?"

Jesus said unto him, "You shall love the Lord your God with all your heart, and with all your soul, and with all your mind." This the first and great commandment. And the second is like it: "You shall love your neighbor as yourself." On these two commandments hang all the Law and the Prophets.

Matthew 22:36–40 (NKJV)

## SECURE THE BLESSINGS OF LIBERTY:

While we are faced with opportunities that transcend our mere imagination to exceed and climb the ladder of success, on the contrary, there are others who are weak and weary. The insignificant feeling is coupled with little or no hope to counter compelling pessimistic emotions and reactions thereof. Doubting any opportunity to walk through an equitable open door to realize life, liberty, and the pursuit of happiness without systematic prejudice. More so, there are zillions of scenarios that encompass journeys that depict life's trails and cycles that are bittersweet. Whatever the reason, God Almighty is the Creator of life and there is liberty in Him. He is the ultimate strength of our joy while meandering through the cycles of life. Winding roads of natural landscapes are curvy; some are bumpy, hilly, rocky, slippery, narrow; high and low dimensions waiting for a disaster to happen if not maneuvered in a deliberate and safe manner.

> "Thy word is a lamp unto my feet, and a light unto my path" (Psalm 119:105).

By the same token, symbolic of spiritual winding roads, navigation comes by the Word of God, which we diligently trust as our spiritual compass, leading to the straight path of justification. Whereas, we must be absent of wavering minds that may cause spiritual catastrophe. On this bittersweet journey, there will be times that blessings seem to overflow. Conversely, other seasons may bring lack (diminishing returns) due to one's imprudent decision making. (Liking to the principle of sowing and reaping.)

But through it all, our sufficiency is in God, be it carnal or spiritual. Having faith in God, "as Abraham believed God and it was accounted to him for righteousness" (Galatians 3:6). Bountiful blessings will flow to the utmost when we walk in divine direction, principle, and unity. As a result, no one will suffer lack.

> And I will make of thee a great nation, and I will bless thee, and make thy name great; and thou shalt be a blessing. And I will bless them that bless thee, and curse him that curseth thee: and in thee shall all families of the earth be blessed.
>
> Genesis 12:2–3

## WORLD OF INTERRELATION

### WE THE WORLD

"WE THE WORLD," full of diversities, disparities with a myriad of parities as a whole. We are interconnected geographically (globally) by commerce/supply chain (economically); communications; technology (World Wide Web) and transportation. Nevertheless, "we the people," in worldview, characteristically have the same makeup—inhaling the breath of life from the supreme Life-Giver; God, our Creator. Life is in the blood (representative of the spiritual connection between God and man) and without it, man will cease to exist.

Over time, as humanity communed with humanity via natural conception, the life-giving blood became tainted through the evil heart/will and quest of man. Thusly, giving way to universal pilgrimage; exhausted with human frailties, little foxes, and adverse actions that threatened our society; i.e., health/welfare, prosperity, and civil liberties. Additionally, political unrest, economic injustices, devastating plagues, climate change, and physical warfare continue to assault our world. Not to mention the insensibility of man's devious acts that threaten opportunities for collaboration and compromise. These unpalatable evil discords infuse and negatively affect the very heart and soul of humanity. Unless the human-race returns to God of the Universe, there will be no peace in the world.

> "These things I have spoken unto you, that in me ye might have peace. In the world ye shall have tribulation: but be of good cheer: I have overcome the world" (John 16:33).

## WE THE PEOPLE OF THE WORLD

"WE THE PEOPLE" of the world have been set free because of the miraculous, unstained blood of Jesus that was shed on Calvary. No more chains (i.e., deprivation—spiritual, physical, financial, emotional, intellectual) can bind our sisters and brothers. The shed blood of Jesus, the Christ, provided equality for all people.

> "If my people, which are called by my name, shall humble themselves, and pray, and seek my face, and turn from their wicked ways; then I will hear from heaven, and will forgive their sin, and will heal their land" (2 Chronicles 7:14).

CHAPTER 6

# Predestined Plan of God

**DIVINE DISCOVERY**

Recorded in the genesis of time, biblical accountability of the Holy Scriptures revealed God's Plan of Divine Discovery.

Humanity's initial journey—all commenced, revealed, and culminated in a divine plot of land. Almighty God, Creator of heaven and earth, subsequent to creating everything in the earth therein, planted a garden eastward in Eden (Garden of Eden), which represented the glorious provision of God. Likewise, God created a man and meticulously placed the man (Adam) there whom he had formed.

> "So, God created man in his own image, in the image of God created he him; male and female created he them" (Genesis 1:27).

This immaculate, beautiful garden was symbolic of a heavenly home for the first fruit of mankind. Adam was placed there to live and thrive. Provided with a variety of herb yielding seed (i.e., fruits, berries), and the fruit tree yielding fruit after its kind were among the food supply. Moreover, specific trees pleasant to the sight and good for food were part of daily bread. As Adam walked in the cool of the day, God's presence (voice) infiltrated the atmosphere, signifying a well of living water to quench every thirst and supply every need.

## DIVINE PLACE

The garden served as the incubator of life, liberty, and was the divine channel for the preordained purpose of humanity. For that cause, Adam was created to live perpetually in an environment that was wholesome and conducive to the plan of God. Notwithstanding, Adam's tasks were to tend the garden, maintain it, and name the animals. Considering this vast responsibility (apart from having daily fellowship with him), in God's infinite wisdom, He knew Adam was still lonely. There was no other creation after his kind, so God made a help meet for him and brought her to Adam (Genesis 2:18, 22). Adam called her "woman" because she was taken out of man. "The rib, which the Lord God had taken from man, made he a woman." It has been noted that "the name given to Eve means to 'breathe, live, or give life.'"[29] By the same token, as expressed earlier in this manuscript, mankind must first develop a wholesome place for purpose to develop and thrive, as sanctioned by God.

## GOD'S DIVINE PURPOSE DISCLOSED

God blessed Adam's hands and Eve's womb and said to them, "Be fruitful and multiply; and replenish the earth, and subdue it: and have dominion over the fish of the sea, and over the fowl of the air, and over every living thing that moveth upon the earth" (Genesis 1:28). In our lives, more often than not, there is a piercing—like a nagging sensation equated to a pointed spirit of unrest when God attempts to get one's attention. It probes the heart of the soul. (Of course, there are many variables associated with this attention-getter.) However, at whatever time, mankind must be intentional about seeking God's purpose for his/her lives. As one's mindset embraces and aligns with the gifts and/or calling, etc. that are revealed, and proper adjustments are made, purpose will be accompanied with a passion to fulfill the God-given blessings within.

## GOD'S ORDER

By providential design, the Tree of Life and the Tree of Knowledge of Good and Evil were placed in the midst of the garden. Thereby, Adam was given permission (by God) to eat freely of every tree of the garden except the Tree of Knowledge of Good and Evil. In the day the commandment is broken, he shall surely die. There stood, as well, the Tree of Life that represents longevity (immortality). Adversely, the Tree of Knowledge of Good and Evil represents choice. By discovering autonomy in decision-making, we ultimately unlock the door of opportunity to choose good or buckle down to evil discretions and ill-fate. The life cycle is full of decisions. Without a doubt, bad choices symbolize dark days ahead; whereas ethical choices symbolize sunny days in the making.

And if it seems evil unto you to serve the LORD, choose you this day whom ye will serve; whether the gods which your fathers served that were on the other side of the flood, or the gods of the Amorites, in whose land ye dwell: but as for me and my house, we will serve the LORD.

Joshua 24:15

CHAPTER 7

# Dusk to Dawn

SONdown

## DIVINE PURSUIT/FORFEITED
## (THE BUD—FALL OF MAN)

Exercising freedom of choice and an imaginative quest to explore the unknown, the serpent beguiled Eve to eat of the forbidden fruit, attempting to abort God's divine purpose while demonizing destiny. Unfortunately, Eve gave the fruit to Adam. Without hesitation, Adam ate of his own volition, even though he had received the commandment from God not to partake of it. The very moment the bittersweet bite was taken was the moment, in time, the sin nature of humanity was birthed (exposed). Subsequently, physical death reared its ugly head. Due to the corruptible nature of Adam, an inherently dark cloud of mortality was ushered into the human anatomy. Over time, the human lifespan would deteriorate slowly and meticulously. Consequently, leaving a lifespan blueprint for all people (individually), and charting brevity versus longevity. Mortality? Appointment time? Maybe short/long, who knows, but God. Whether it is slow or progressive signifies time is at hand.

Eating the forbidden fruit opened Adam and Eve's mortal eyes, and they sensed they were naked and exposed. Instantaneously, this event imperiled humanity's existence and so sentenced mankind to a wilderness walk. Regrettably, Adam and Eve's intellectual knack rested on yielding to their carnal will rather than spiritual consciousness (sacred place/mindset). By doing so, they aborted God's divine plan and purpose, which caused them to sacrifice their spiritual fellowship; they embraced spiritual and physical death, jilting their divine place with God.

## PARADISE LOST

As a result of disobedience and irresponsibility, their eyes were opened, and they were ultimately expelled from the Garden of Paradise. Subsequently, upon their exodus, Adam and Eve were forced to chart their own course independently in the absence of the covering of God. Sadly, when Adam and Eve were cast out of the garden, they left behind foundational resources (spiritual and natural) that only God could give. Due to their abrupt departure, they were no longer able to enjoy spiritual communion with God and their agricultural habitation in its perfect state. The celestial atmosphere that permeated the garden and the sweet-smelling nature of the presence of God faded into dreadful reality.

The agents of fallen mankind journeyed in discovering the barren place. Their way was cursed and rendered a journey experience filled with turbulent conditions, thereby igniting a toxic circle of moral, physical, and economical blight as sin memorializes darkness. Their onward itinerary was an unknown rainy, rocky, desert land void of the good life that was provided while they were inhabitants in the garden. The exodus from the garden is a testament to Adam and Eve's imprudence that culminated in the vexation of Spirit! Sorry to say, change in their dwelling place and the curse imposed upon humanity through their waywardness wreaked pain, suffering, and immeasurable hardship (i.e., childbearing unto death, work by tilling of the soil, sweat of the brow); and, as you know, hardly any rest.

> "Man, that is born of a woman is of few days and full of trouble" (Job 14:1).

Due to this depravity, humanity was symbolically thrust onto the natural artery (as mentioned earlier). Humanity's life journey took on the sin nature of Adam and Eve and became the first big issue of life, thereby, (by popular vote) casting the effect of being railroaded. Sadly, forced into the midst of life's throes beyond peoples' (progeny/Adam/Eve) control. Outcome: condemnation/mortality. Many people remain skeptics, joke, and have misgivings regarding this chain of events. Besides, "we the people" of the world are given the opportunity to choose the Tree of Life. Let us not forget, just like Adam and Eve, "we the people" (prior to divine transformation) have no clothes on; stripped naked and exposed to the Tree of Knowledge of Good and Evil (choices). Now the bittersweet fruit is on our natural route (be it carnal or spiritual) to cherry-pick (choose).

> "This is what the LORD says: 'Stand at the crossroads and look; ask for the ancient paths, ask where the good way is, and walk in it, and you will

find rest for your souls. But you said, 'We will not walk in it'" (Jeremiah 6:16, NIV).

God's ordained plan is to allow humanity the right to choose. Not to serve as a robot, but to serve willingly in love. No, humanity was not railroaded but placed in a position to be blessed and to partake of the God-given provisions and promises inherent in becoming a Child of God (believer). Be wary not to forfeit the blessings and sojourn on the broad path void of a divine harvest.

> "Wherefore the rather, brethren, give diligence to make your calling and election sure: for if ye do these things, ye shall never fall" (2 Peter 1:10).

Again, as Daddy oftentimes quoted, "The bud will have a bitter taste sweeter will be the flower."

## SONRISE

## HOPE OF GLORY
## (THE FLOWER/JESUS, THE RISEN SAVIOR)

Through Adam and Eve's progeny, the earth's population increased as generations multiplied. And as each generation begat the other (Genesis 5:1–10; Matthew 1:1–25), as in Matthew, the lineage of Abraham, Isaac, and Jacob by way of King David, inclusive of the immaculate conception of Jesus, the Christ, blossomed as the sweet-smelling Savior, the Flower.

> "Now the birth of Jesus Christ was on this wise: When as his mother Mary was espoused to Joseph, before they came together, she was found with child of the Holy Ghost" (Matthew 1:18).

Humankind was drowning in bitter darkness, and the foul fragrance of disloyalty and corruptible behavior infiltrated the earth, producing an unfruitful land. Nevertheless, because of God's unconditional love, mankind was given a way to escape spiritual separation and deprivation; by reclaiming glorious inheritance as joint heirs with Jesus Christ. The emancipating Blood of Jesus made atonement for humanity's sin, transcending from dusk to dawn. In journeying the spiritual path, Jesus Christ is the throughway and supreme artery; the redemptive path to salvation.

> "Jesus saith unto him, I am the way, the truth, and the life: no man cometh unto the Father, but by me" (John 14:6).

## PRELUDE TO SALVATION

The predestined journey (primary spiritual artery) led Jesus to Mount Calvary (up Golgotha's hill) where the death, burial, and resurrection of our Lord and Savior, Jesus Christ, is memorialized. It is a testament of the glorious pathway of new life, liberty, justification, sanctification, transformation, and prosperity. The Blood of Jesus cleansed all unrighteousness and will never lose its miraculous power. Jesus, "...which taketh away the sin of the world" (John 1:29 ), made a way to escape (coming down through forty-two generations) and consecrated a place (for humanity) that no man can replace.

As an obedient servant, "for the people," Jesus laid down His life and surrendered to the cross. Gloriously raised on the third day, He annihilated sin, encrypted as darkness. His divine itinerary was the route from heaven to earth; cross to the grave; grave to hell; third-day ascension from earth to Glory. Ascending back to heaven where Jesus reoccupied His Holy Place and "...is set down on the right hand of the throne of God" (Hebrews 12:2). With each ordered step, Jesus completed the assigned task (divine purpose) set before Him.

"O death, where is thy sting? O grave, where is thy victory?" (1 Corinthians 15:55).

"Wherefore he saith, when he ascended up on high, he led captivity captive, and gave gifts unto men" (Ephesians 4:8).

His loving sacrificial offering opened the door to salvation for all mankind and is given liberally to those who believe.

> Therefore, doth my Father love me, because I lay down my life, that I might take it again. No man taketh it from me, but I lay it down of myself. I have power to lay it down, and I have power to take it again.
>
> John 10:17–18

> For God so loved the world, that he gave his only begotten Son, that whosoever believeth in him should not perish, but have everlasting life.
>
> John 3:16

Just as God gave Adam the commandment requiring obedience, He has given the commandment (requiring obedience) to humankind. "We the people" have the same opportunity to yield our vessel (body), herewith choosing good vs. evil. As the winding roads of life unfold, culminating with journey's end, the conscionable aspect of life's pathway results in the place of choice. Be it by deliberate constructive measures or careless declaration of action taken, we would have landed where we purposed.

> "For all have sinned, and come short of the Glory of God" (Romans 3:23).

"The Lord is not slack concerning his promise, as some men count slackness; but is longsuffering to us-ward, **not** willing **that** any should **perish**, but that all should come to repentance" (**2 Peter 3:9**).

## LIFE-ROUSING QUESTIONS

As we trod in this life and make our indelible mark in humanity, life-rousing questions yet remain:

"Who do YOU choose, Twenty-First Century Man and Culturally Modern Day Eve?"
"Jesus or Satan?"

"I am the door. If anyone enters by Me, he will be saved, and will go in and out and find pasture" (John 10:9, NKJV).

"Which one do YOU choose, my brother?"
"Good or Evil?"

"I call heaven and earth as witnesses today against you, that I have set before you, life, and death, blessing and cursing; therefore, choose life, that both you and your descendants may live" (Deuteronomy 30:19, NKJV).

"When will YOU pursue/propel, my sister?"
"Tomorrow may very well be today."

"While it is said, Today, if ye will hear his voice, harden not your hearts, as in the provocation" (Hebrews 3:15).

"Where will YOU land, my brother?"
"Heaven or Hell?"

Sisters/brothers (not in an abyss), but in the Prepared Place.

Divinely Designed by God!

"And since I'm going away to prepare a place for you, I'll come back again and welcome you into my presence, so that you may be where I am" (John 14:3, ISV).

In glorious awaiting for the return of our Lord and Savior, Jesus Christ, our minds are focused and we are endeavoring to be in His presence. Looking to heaven for the starlight (Jesus) that forever illuminates our hearts.

CHAPTER 8

# The Bright and Morning Star

**CROWN OF LIFE BESTOWED**

"I Jesus have sent mine angel to testify unto you these things in the churches. I am the root and the offspring of David, and the bright morning Star" (Revelation 22:16).

"Blessed is the man that endureth temptation: for when he is tried, he shall receive the crown of life, which the Lord hath promised to them that love him" (James 1:12).

Symbolically on a sunshiny day—the moment Believers (born again Christians) accept Christ as Lord and Savior, stillness infiltrates the air (spirit), and the sun (SON) shines radiantly on your face (heart) with a touch of cool breeze in the air (breath of life) infusing your soul. The darkened night (issues of life) dissipates with the hope of glory, celebrating like morning dew to refresh and purify mind, body, spirit, and soul.

> "We have also a more-sure word of prophecy; whereunto ye do well that ye take heed, as unto a light that shineth in a dark place, until the day dawn, and the day star arise in your hearts" (2 Peter 1:19).

In Discovering Our Divine Place, we will sit at the welcome table and partake of this Holy Bread (Word of God). Ultimately, we become the Redeemed (Bittersweet Flower) in the new Jerusalem where "we the people" shall reside there perpetually and be with the Lord. We would have said goodbye to a darkened world, rooted and transitioned into His glorious light.

> "These are they which came out of great tribulation, and have **washed their robes, and made them white** in the blood of the Lamb" (Revelation 7:14).

> "And I John saw the holy city, new Jerusalem, coming down from God out of heaven, prepared as a bride adorned for her husband" (Revelation 21:2).

## POEM:
## "WE THE WORLD"

We are the world
Simply put, we are the people.

Ascending to be all that we can be
and striving for perfection in a grandiose way.

Not descending to what we used to be
realizing our soul is not free until we bow down to Thee.

The world was formed by the Hand of God
and presented to Adam in the garden.
Everything was perfect, it and man,
until Satan made his grandstand.

Instead of resisting, Adam subdued
and bowed down to Satan's stool.

The price was high, and the cost was great
forced him out of the golden gate.

His place of comfort, provision, and purpose made void
and by a sinful act, forfeited the yard.

Cherubic angels of fire were standing on guard
to ensure that Adam would not make another mark.

Because of Adam, we all made mistakes
(Born in sin and shaped in inequity)
but God made a way for us to escape.

By God's grace, He sent His only begotten Son
to prepare a place; the battle is already won.

A place for all, we the world and all they that dwell therein
have created an opened door and are invited in.

Just knock with the drumbeat of your heart
Tenacity of your spirit giving you a fresh start.

Reach out and touch the world with your soul
engaging mankind as a whole.

This world will be a better place
If we love one another and give GOD the praise.

Hence, the greatest story has already been told
Jesus, our Savior cru-ci-fied
laid down His life so we can survive.

Get ready to receive HIM because HE shall return
on that great day,
Oh, how our hearts yearn.

Believers get ready to meet Him in the air;
our Lord and Savior will meet you there.

# Epilogue

From the concept of MY place, YOUR place, and OUR place, the vital ongoing objective is that "we the people" genuinely collaborate (i.e., spiritually, relationally, economically, etc.) in finding common ground in advancing individually, as a community, and as a nation/world— realizing that some bittersweet experiences may perhaps stimulate steppingstones to impel positive change.

> "But you are a chosen generation, a royal priesthood, a holy nation, His own special people, that you may proclaim the praises of Him who called you out of darkness into his marvelous light" (1 Peter 2:9, NKJV).

On the contrary, from all perspectives, divine place and purpose possibly will be delayed indefinitely without a deliberate attempt to pursue. Or, ultimately, aborted without ever reaching fruition. Alas, if this occurs, it will be due to a barren spirit unwilling to embrace a providential ending.

> "But the natural man receiveth not the things of the Spirit of God, for they are foolishness unto him; neither can he know them, because they are spiritually discerned" (1 Corinthians 2:14).

**Discovering MY place:**

The genesis of my startling journey mirrors the threat of a fatal birth that triumphed over becoming a born-again Christian. As I strolled along life's path, at some point in my adult years, spiritual maturity began to develop, conforming me to a devoted Christian until this day. As spiritual maturity unveiled, I discovered that spiritual development alone comes with its own enduring threats, challenges, and decisions.

> "Therefore, I take pleasure in infirmities, in reproaches, in necessities, in persecutions, in distresses for Christ's sake: for when I am weak, then am I strong" (1 Corinthians 12:10).

Filled with God's blessings of marriage for over thirty years, Neal and I continue to serve as Ministers of the Gospel, etc. Being deliberate in consistently consecrating my place reinforces me to walk out my divine purpose/assignments according to God's will and yet declare, all things are working for my good.

"Commit your works to the LORD, And your thoughts will be established" (Proverbs 16:3, NKJV).

"I will praise You, O LORD, with all my whole heart; I will tell of all Your marvelous works" (Psalm 9:1, NKJV).

Moreover, during my early elementary school years, poetic inspirations were embedded in my spirit. Periodically, I began phrasing and penning, on paper simplistic thoughts into poems as a pastime endeavor. That pastime activity continued until my adolescent years, which generated new interests, aspirations, and challenges. Over the years, that creativity never ceased to exist.

**Discovering YOUR place:**

For individuals who are contemplating making positive adjustments, a willing mind is essential to propel in reaching your divine purpose. Stay focused on the prize (Jesus), and the promises and principles in the Word of God. Your spiritual altitude is predicated on how high you decide (choose) to reach. Embrace your assignment. Also, hold fast to the window of opportunities and possibilities to seek the *greater* in you. Remember: With man, you walk alone. With God, He is always by your side. If, by chance, you feel like giving up, allow Jesus to carry you.

In moving forward, it would be a disservice for anyone to neglect their predestined assignment. As a result, you may perhaps end up in lack, as the prodigal son: defamed (character); deserted (friends); denied (necessities); dejected (contentment); and deprived (love). Likewise, as soon as the prodigal son came to himself and realized the fun and folly were temporary fixes, he made the necessary adjustments and his outcome was blessed. You must truly realize:

a) Your character is more precious than silver and gold (Proverbs 22:1).
b) Jesus will never abandon you (Hebrews 13:5).
c) There is no lack in God (Psalm 34:9).
d) There is no need to worry (Joshua 1:9).
e) God's love is absolute/unconditional (1 John 4:19).

Your measured steps will be in providential order, sanctioned for a blessed life.

"Ye did run well; who did hinder you that ye should not obey the truth?" (Galatians 5:7).

Mature Christians, at this juncture, your pace should be steady. Endurance: powerful and home-run sure. Bottom of the Stretch! You are dressed for battle knowing "No weapon formed against you shall prosper" (Isaiah 54:17, NKJV). Without delay, you are suited to run the race that is before you with all diligence and patience. While the stairway to heaven becomes intimately closer, stride becomes absolutely deliberate; divine destiny is significantly secure when devoting to choosing the straight path. As you continue to make progress in your Christian walk, consistency with respect to wholesomeness is paramount. To accomplish the prescribed spiritual paradigm, the prudent thing is to continue to maintain a consecrated mindset and an environment rid of varied influences that will sabotage the spirit of excellence. Strive to be influential to those who have not yet committed to this spiritual benchmark.

As a believer, in the event your spiritual gifts, talents, creativity are compromised in any way, these virtues will suffer loss. To behave in this vein will create a spiritual stumbling-block. Altogether, you are disallowing the Power and Divine Fragrance of God to do, in the spirit, what man cannot do in the flesh. Notwithstanding, the effectiveness of your position and/or presentation will be deemed superficial and/or spiritually discerned. Without an intentional effort to address and come into corrective alignment, the anointing oil of excellence will become dismal. Consequently, your undertaking turns into a sounding brass and tingling cymbal, void of God's anointing. Attempting to survive or serve, in any capacity, without Almighty God can be symbolized by a cruise ship without an anchor incapable of docking.

> "But the one who looks into the perfect law, the law of liberty, and perseveres, being no hearer who forgets but a doer who acts, he will be blessed in his doing" (James 1:25, ESV).

**Discovering OUR place:**

"We the people" must continually go beyond what is and what has been and get back to basics. The common denominator for having a more perfect union is love. Essential footing is needed in walking this Christian journey. This principle will suffer lack without: a) Spiritual circumcision of the heart; b) Meticulous sacrifice; c) Consistent prayer; d) Collaboration; and e) Perseverance. These ethics are vital for the common good of all.

Briefing of ethics is as follows:

a) Spiritual circumcision of the heart—regeneration (rebirth, renewal/heart of the mind); cutting away (discontinue) anything that is not like God; old things are passed away and behold all things become new with the love of God;

b) Meticulous sacrifice—selflessness; intentional empathy toward others (caring and sharing);

c) Consistent prayer—pray without ceasing/wavering (with a purpose);
d) Collaboration—(relational) involves communication, listening, understanding, compromise;
e) Perseverance—Be steadfast; keep moving...Trust God and He will meet the need.

To Rise Up, with anticipation, the Heads of State (governing body) must be genuinely willing to regroup, embrace, and uphold the ordinances outlined in the Constitution of the United States without partisan partition (encompassing all jurisdictions). Yes, for some, this effort may appear to be an unattainable desire or stretch, given the current partisan state of affairs. But as for believers, we know that all things are possible with God. Nevertheless, make no mistake about it, this great proclamation was founded on the Word of God.

> "Live in harmony with one another. Do not be haughty, but associate with the lowly. Never be wise in your own sight" (Romans 12:16, ESV).

Collectively, with spiritual circumcision, this endeavor can be realized when "we the people" turn over the soil of divisiveness and purposely begin to sow peace lilies within ourselves and others. We must irrigate sincere harmony across the board by developing trust and renewal, constructive actions, and resolve.

> "If ye be willing and obedient, ye shall eat the good of the land: But if ye refuse and rebel, ye shall be devoured with the sword: for the mouth of the Lord hath spoken it" (Isaiah 1:19–20).

**Predestined PLAN of God:**

God's redemptive plan illuminated a darkened world by SONrays likened to the Bright and Morning Star. Jesus' predestined purpose was to disrobe His divine nature and holy place in heaven to take on the sin of the world (humanity) as God-man. As Redeemer, and precious Lamb of God, Jesus freely left His heavenly home (place). While on His ordained journey, at the appointed time, took humanity's place on the cross where He bled/died, and became the ultimate sacrifice.

> "God made him who had no sin to be sin for us, so that in him we might become the righteousness of God" (2 Corinthians 5:21, NIV).

> "And being found in appearance as a man, he humbled himself by becoming obedient to death—even death on a cross!" (Philippians 2:8, NIV).

By Jesus walking out His divine assignment, this supreme sacrifice guaranteed salvation (unmerited gift) for those who believed. This was the only way for humanity to be forgiven of sin and be reunited with God.

Now is the time! Mankind has a prime opportunity to reclaim a glorious inheritance. Forfeiting this blessing will result in abiding in a dreadful place, absent of eternal rest in God's heavenly home.

In this present age, "we the people" have the same privilege and opportunity to choose between the Tree of Life or the Tree of Knowledge of Good and Evil. As we grow in grace, let us embrace the prescribed course and walk therein. While embarking on this endeavor, it is time to take to the wings of love and fly. Preordained purpose comes to fruition, embodying the clarion call (charge) with gifts, talents, and creativity. With fervor, "we the people" have a call to fulfill our destined assignment, which will be such a blessing to humanity. All glory be to God, as we go forward, in excellency, walking out our divine purpose by establishing our divine place as a bittersweet flower.

Go in Peace.

# Endnotes

1. *Vocabulary.com Dictionary*, s.v. "bittersweet," accessed April 30, 2024, https://www.vocabulary.com/dictionary/bittersweet.
2. "New All-American Roads, National Scenic Byways Designated in National Forests." 2013. US Forest Service. 2013. https://www.fs.usda.gov/about-agency/newsroom/releases/new-all-american-roads-national-scenic-byways-designated-national.
3. "Cultural Heritage." 2016. US Forest Service. July 29, 2016. https://www.fs.usda.gov/managing-land/heritage.
4. National Geographic. 2023. "Landscape | National Geographic Society." Education.nationalgeographic.org. 2023. https://education.nationalgeographic.org/resource/landscape/.
5. Publishers, HarperCollins. n.d. "The American Heritage Dictionary Entry: Artery." Www.ahdictionary.com. Accessed May 2, 2024. https://www.ahdictionary.com/word/search.html?q=artery.
6. Wigglesworth, Shelley. 2021. "Bittersweet Vine |

Is the Invasive Plant Friend or Foe?" New England. November 1, 2021. https://newengland.com/living/gardening/bittersweet-vine-friend-or-foe/.

7 "Definition of Decisiveness | Dictionary.com." 2019. Www.dictionary.com. 2019. https://www.dictionary.com/browse/decisiveness.

8 "Indecisive." n.d. The Free Dictionary. Accessed May 21, 2024. https://www.thefreedictionary.com/indecisive.

9 "The God-Shaped Vacuum – OAC." n.d. https://oacvancouver.ca/the-god-shaped-vacuum/.

10 "What Is the Inner Man?" n.d. GotQuestions.org. https://www.gotquestions.org/inner-man.html.

11 "Difference between Mind and Soul." 2011. Difference Between. March 8, 2011. http://www.differencebetween.net/language/difference-between-mind-and-soul/#ixzz8asZDvMbB.

12 "Definition of ROLLER COASTER." 2024. Merriam-Webster.com. April 26, 2024. https://www.merriam-webster.com/dictionary/roller%20coaster.

13 "Christian Ministry." 2022. Wikipedia. June 28, 2022. https://en.wikipedia.org/wiki/Christian_ministry.

14 "Purpose Definition & Meaning | Britannica Dictionary." n.d. Www.britannica.com. https://www.britannica.com/dictionary/purpose.

15 "What Is Predestination? Is Predestination Biblical?" n.d. GotQuestions.org. https://www.

gotquestions.org/predestination.html.
16 "King James Bible Dictionary - Reference List - Purpose." n.d. King James Bible Dictionary. Accessed May 1, 2024. https://www.kingjamesbibledictionary.com/Dictionary/purpose.
17 "Definition of PROPEL." n.d. Www.merriam-Webster.com. https://www.merriam-webster.com/dictionary/propel.
18 "What Is the Implication of 'Eye of the Storm'?" n.d. English Language & Usage Stack Exchange. Accessed May 2, 2024. https://english.stackexchange.com/questions/42195/what-is-the-implication-of-eye-of-the-storm.
19 Greear, J. D. 2021. "Should Christians Accept Culture or Reject It?" JD Greear Ministries. September 6, 2021. https://jdgreear.com/should-christians-accept-culture-or-reject-it/.
20 "Weather-The-Storm Definition & Meaning | YourDictionary." n.d. Www.yourdictionary.com. Accessed May 2, 2024. https://www.yourdictionary.com/weather-the-storm.
21 Cambridge Dictionary. 2024. "Weather the Storm." @CambridgeWords. May 2024. https://dictionary.cambridge.org/us/dictionary/english/weather-the-storm.
22 "Dictionary.com | Meanings & Definitions of English Words." n.d. Dictionary.com. https://www.dictionary.com/browse/obtain.

23 "Responsibility." 2019. TheFreeDictionary. com. 2019. https://www.thefreedictionary.com/responsibility.
24 "Endurability Definition & Meaning | YourDictionary." n.d. Www.yourdictionary.com. Accessed May 21, 2024. https://www.yourdictionary.com/endurability.
25 "Definition of ENDURANCE." n.d. Www.merriam-Webster.com. https://www.merriam-webster.com/dictionary/endurance.
26 "The Article of the U.S. Constitution." n.d. National Constitution Center – Constitutioncenter.org. https://constitutioncenter.org/the-constitution/preamble#:~:text=We%20the%20People%20of%20the.
27 "Union with Christ Meaning - Bible Definition and References." n.d. Bible Study Tools. Accessed May 2, 2024. https://www.biblestudytools.com/dictionary/union-with-christ/.
28 Wikipedia Contributors. 2019. "Agape." Wikipedia. Wikimedia Foundation. September 22, 2019. https://en.wikipedia.org/wiki/Agape.
29 Norén, Hannah. 2023. "Women, Be Life-Givers." The Gospel Coalition | Norden. May 1, 2023. https://norden.thegospelcoalition.org/article/women-be-life-givers/.

# Bibliography

*The American Heritage Dictionary of the English Language.* 2016. Boston: Houghton Mifflin Harcourt.

"Assimilation - WordReference.com Dictionary of English." n.d. Www.wordreference.com. Accessed May 3, 2024. https://www.wordreference.com/definition/assimilation.

Bible Study Tools. 2019. "Read & Study the Bible - Daily Verse, Scripture by Topic, Stories." Bible Study Tools. 2019. https://www.biblestudytools.com/.

Bowden, John. 2005. *Encyclopedia of Christianity.* New York, N.Y.: Oxford University Press.

Cambridge Dictionary. 2019. "Cambridge English Dictionary: Definitions & Meanings." Cambridge.org. 2019. https://dictionary.cambridge.org/us/dictionary/english/.

"Christian Ministry." 2022. Wikipedia. June 28, 2022.

https://en.wikipedia.org/wiki/Christian_ministry.

Dictionary.com. 2024. "Dictionary.com." Dictionary. com. Dictionary.com. 2024. https://www.dictionary. com/.

"English Language & Usage Stack Exchange." 2019. English Language & Usage Stack Exchange. 2019. https://english.stackexchange.com/.

Farlex. 2019. "Dictionary, Encyclopedia and Thesaurus - the Free Dictionary." TheFreeDictionary.com. 2019. https://www.thefreedictionary.com/.

Got Questions Ministries. n.d. "GQM: Got Questions Ministries." GQM.one. Accessed May 3, 2024. https://www.gqm.one/.

"King James Bible Dictionary - Online Edition." n.d. King James Bible Dictionary. https:// kingjamesbibledictionary.com/.

"LoveToKnowMedia – LoveToKnowMedia." n.d. Www. lovetoknowmedia.com. Accessed May 3, 2024. https://www.lovetoknowmedia.com/.

Merriam-Webster. 2024. "Merriam-Webster Dictionary." Merriam-Webster.com. Merriam-

Webster. 2024. https://www.merriam-webster.com/.

National Archives. 2018. "The Constitution of the United States." National Archives. The U.S. National Archives and Records Administration. November 16, 2018. https://www.archives.gov/founding-docs/constitution.

National Constitution Center. 2018. "Home - National Constitution Center." National Constitution Center – Constitutioncenter.org. 2018. https://constitutioncenter.org/.

National Geographic. 2023. "Landscape | National Geographic Society." Education. nationalgeographic.org. 2023. https://education.nationalgeographic.org/resource/landscape/.

"Oriental Bittersweet: An Aggressive, Invasive Plant." 2015. MSU Extension. 2015. https://www.canr.msu.edu/news/oriental_bittersweet_an_aggressive_invasive_plant.

English Dictionary. 2023. "Oxford English Dictionary." OED.com. Oxford University Press. 2023. https://www.oed.com/.

Thinkmap. 2019. "Find out How Strong Your Vocabulary Is and Learn New Words at Vocabulary.com." Vocabulary.com. 2019. https://www.vocabulary.com/.

"Top 25 Quotes by Blaise Pascal (of 727)." n.d. A-Z Quotes. Accessed May 3, 2024. https://www.azquotes.com/author/11361-Blaise_Pascal#google_vignette.

U.S. Forest Service. 2019. "Home | US Forest Service." Usda.gov. December 5, 2019. https://www.fs.usda.gov/.

Wikipedia Contributors. 2019. "Agape." Wikipedia. Wikimedia Foundation. September 22, 2019. https://en.wikipedia.org/wiki/Agape.

Printed in the USA
CPSIA information can be obtained
at www.ICGtesting.com
CBHW071547090824
12912CB00008B/109